THE WORLD'S MOST

AMAZING MYSTERIES

Dad

THE WORLD'S MOST
AMAZING
MYSTERIES

BY
NIGEL BLUNDELL

SUNBURST BOOKS

PHOTOGRAPHY CREDITS

Express Newspapers plc: 16, 25, 125.
Paris-Match: 46.
Leo Dickinson, Rex Pictures: 95.
United Press International: 128.
Associated Press: 135 (top).
Frank Searle: 135 (bottom).
Pictorial Press: 146.
Square Circle Archives: 166 (bottom).
South West Pictures Bristol: 179.
Copyright unknown: 91, 93, 107, 127, 166 (top).

Copyright text © Nigel Blundell 1995
Copyright design © Sunburst Books 1995

This edition published 1995 by Sunburst Books, Deacon House,
65 Old Church Street, London SW3 5BS

ISBN 1 85778 063 9

Printed and bound in the United Kingdom

Contents

Introduction

Man has explored every corner of the earth and plumbed the depths of the oceans. He has tamed the wildernesses and learned to forecast and sometimes control the elements. Historians have neatly parcelled up our past, analysts have explained the complexities of the present, and scientists have predicted the future. Homo sapiens has an answer for everything. Or so he would like to think!

Yet, as man's knowledge increases, a strange counter-balance seems to occur. For every question he answers, another is raised. For every mystery solved, a new one emerges. This enigmatic universe keeps throwing up fresh mysteries to taunt our academic knowledge and scientific expertise.

How can a perfectly healthy person simply burst into flame? How can a king's curse reach from beyond the grave?

Gathered together in *The World's Most Amazing Mysteries* are questions that have tested man's knowledge and tantalised his imagination over the years. They continue to fascinate.

The stories in this book, however, beat the plots of any thriller. For these are mysteries no writer could make up – and which no reader has ever solved!

Noah's Ark

Did the Great Deluge ever happen? Did Noah's Ark ever exist? Was Noah, as described in the Book of Genesis, instructed by God to build the Ark and to fill it with animals to replenish the earth after the flood waters had subsided? Over the centuries, many people, from religious fanatics to professional archaeologists, claim to have solved the secret.

Accounts of the Flood and the Ark are not confined to the Bible. Research indicates that the deluge may actually have happened, and that at some time during human history, the world was swamped with a flood the like of which has never been seen since. Certainly eastern cultures – not just the Bible – have written records of the great deluge, and while the mystery remains as to whether these accounts are of legendary or real events, there is a body of evidence which substantiates the argument that at some time in human history a great flood did take place.

The first mention of a deluge engulfing the world comes in *The Epic of Gilgamesh*, a Babylonian work transcribed in the seventh century. It corresponds with the better-known Hebrew version recording Noah and his Ark, except that in this account the rains did not last forty days and forty nights, but seven. This, coupled with the Ark legend, and an Armenian text chronicling a similar event, has inspired archaeologists to try to find concrete evidence that a flood occurred.

In 1929 Sir Leonard Woolley, an eminent archaeologist of his day, discovered at the ancient Sumerian city of Ur in Iraq some 3.6 metres of thick clay. He declared: 'So vast a mass of silt laid at one time could only be the result of a very great flood.' He dated the clay as having been deposited around 3500 BC.

Unfortunately, other eminent men decried his theory, pointing out the absence of evidence for a great flood at nearby sites – and the fact that Ur itself survived, indication that the flood was hardly the wholesale wiping-out of people and animals described in the Bible.

Other sites in Iraq have been visited over the years by archaeologists, particularly one at Kish. But again, the remains of the houses indicated that, although damaged by water, they were quite strong enough to withstand that particular deluge. These were, it is now generally assumed, local floods on a relatively small scale.

Excavation of Mesopotamian sites proved nothing. But a prayer from 2200 BC, discovered earlier this century, records a chilling event: 'Waters pouring out – destroying cities like the flood wave.' This, say the believers, is one more piece of evidence that the deluge did take place.

As proof of Noah's existence, those who believe the Great Deluge did actually occur point out the strange findings on Mount Ararat, the place where the Ark is supposed to have come to rest after the waters subsided.

The mountain, soaring 5,165 metres above a flat plain, 965 kilometres east of the Turkish city of Ankara, has been scoured from base to summit in search of clues for the Ark. It is a bleak, snow-capped mountain at the top of which it would be difficult to breathe without oxygen. Nevertheless, priests of the fifth century record that they managed to climb it, scraped bitumen-coated wood from the remains of the Ark and brought it back.

More puzzling still are the timber fragments which have been found on Mount Ararat by successive Ark investigators. The timber is of a type that does not come from trees growing in the region. It has been identified as 4000-year-old wood, originating from the plains of Mesopotamia – where Noah is said to have lived.

The first pieces were retrieved by Victorian archaeologists, eager to reinforce Christian theories about the Ark. In 1969 the French industrialist Fernand Navarra, who had led an earlier expedition in 1955, returned to find further wood samples. Thanks to the advances in the science of carbon dating, he came up with an amazing result.

Carbon dating is a most accurate way of estimating the age of objects, whether they are natural of man-made. Everything contains natural radioactivity, and the radioactivity in the carbon all organic materials contain decays at a known rate. By measuring the radioactivity in the carbon in anything from ash trees to zebra bones, a precise dating can be obtained.

Navarra determined that the wood on Mount Ararat was dated at 3,500 years BC!

Previous souvenir hunters included archaeologist Lord Bryce, who found a large chunk of wood (from the ship's hull, he surmised) in 1876. And a prominent Russian researcher 50 years before him mapped out the snub-nose peak of the mountain – flat enough, he thought, for a vessel to beach itself there once the flood waters had ebbed away.

What of the vessel itself? Could a ship so large as to take so many creatures 'two by two' have been constructed? Yes, say the Bible-believers. But the Biblical dimensions of the craft are truly enormous – it was said to be 300 cubits long, 50 broad and 30 high. This would put the Ark at 146 m long, 22.8 m broad and 13.7 m high. A vessel, in fact, displacing 43,688 tonnes, with over 1.4 million square metres of deck space!

That, say 'Arkaeologists', would have provided ample room for the creatures Noah took on the voyage and would still have left plenty of room for himself and his family. Those who scoff at the notion of such a craft, and all the problems it would entail in terms of its construction and the sailing and navigation skills required to set forth in it, can only be reminded of the impressive knowledge of seafaring which ancient civilisations possessed – proved by artefacts such as the papyrus boats of Ancient Egyptians that were capable of mammoth voyages across the oceans.

There is one further theory of a Great Deluge: that the world was plunged beneath the waves, but long before any written records were kept.

Some scientists say that the submersion happened in the Stone Age, and may not have been so much a flood as a gradual upsurge in the level of the seas over years, perhaps caused by some colossal natural disaster of as yet unknown.

Was it distant memories of just such an upheaval that are responsible for the stories in the Bible and elsewhere? Whatever the origins of the story of the Great Deluge, no one will ever be able to disprove that Noah and his Ark really did exist.

Stonehenge

Few relics of the ancient world are as mystifying as the great standing pillars of Stonehenge. These megaliths of ancient man defy belief: how did they get there, what is their purpose, where did the technology to erect them come from?

Across the centuries, the giant, brooding stones of this awe-inspiring ruin have stood as a challenge to man's knowledge of himself and his ancient world. Despite every theory they still keep their secrets. For they are made from rocks only found hundreds of miles from Stonehenge. How were the stones transported? How was this engineering miracle performed? And above all, why?

Stonehenge is but one cluster in a swathe of gigantic monumental rocks which stretches around Europe and the British Isles, from as far north as the Shetland Islands to Malta in the south. There are around 900 sites of standing stones in Britain alone. But Stonehenge, rising above the flat plateau of Salisbury Plain, is easily the most famous of them. Indeed, among all the great stone sites of Europe, Stonehenge remains unique because of the sophisticated way that the blocks appear to have been designed to fit one another and to form a carefully complete whole.

It is only relatively recently that archaeologists have been prepared to say that these great stones may have been the constructed by advanced astronomers or mathematicians rather than barbarians and savages. Much astute detective work has resulted in extraordinary theories on the origin and history of the megaliths (the word is Greek for 'great stones') which should not be dismissed lightly.

Stonehenge was built in three distinct stages, spanning a period of over 1000 years. Each group of people who began the mammoth task did not quite finish it, leaving the legacy of completion to the succeeding generations.

The first builders were Neolithic, working on the site around 2700 BC. It was they who set up the encircling ditch and bank and the heel stone, which is aligned so that the first rays of light from the sun on midsummer's day strike both it and the central point of the two stone circles. These same people created the 56 shallow pits called the Aubrey Holes – named after the writer who discovered them – which form a ring just inside the bank, and which when excavated were found to contain bones and cremated objects.

Some 800 years on, the men and women whom we call the Beaker People because of their habit of burying ornate artefacts of pottery with their dead, moved in on the site. They, by means

Modern day Druids worship the Summer Solstice at the ancient and mystical monument of Stonehenge.

unknown, accomplished one of the truly great engineering feats of all time. In an age when tools were made of flint and bone and the wheel had not yet been invented, they hewed rock from the Prescelly Hills in South Wales and transported it the 480 kilometres to the site we now know as Stonehenge. The 80 mammoth bluestones, each weighing more than four tons, were then assembled into a double circle inside the enclosure built earlier.

Around 1500 BC, the builders of the third Stonehenge again brought in massive boulders, this time from the Marlborough Downs, probably dragged to the site on primitive sledges by upwards of 1000 men. The individual boulders weighed more than 50 tons each, and were hewn from Sarsen rock, one of the hardest minerals. After the arduous journey, they were fashioned into the shapes which now stand like gaunt sentinels on the bleak, windswept plain.

Finally, a people who could not read or write or fashion a wheel devised a system to put the huge stone lintels on top of the upright stones. In addition, the builders of Stonehenge shared something with the prehistoric builders at other sites around Europe – all these monuments are constructed using the same unit of measurement, a unit archaeologists have come to call the megalithic yard: a distance of 0.83 metres. No one has yet been able to explain either how or why this common unit could have come to be used by so many distant peoples of the time.

Although the strange cult of the modern Druids, or Celtic Priests, now lays claim to Stonehenge, experts believe that it is far too old to have been constructed by their Celtic forerunners. So which cult and which men were behind the megalithic mystery?

Theories about the structure abound, but perhaps the one expounded by Oxford University professor Alexander Thom bears the most credence. In 1934, after a hard day's sailing, Professor Thom took his boat into Lock Roag on the Isle of Lewis, off Scotland's bleak west coast. Silhouetted against the rising full moon were the standing stones of Callanish, Scotland's Stonehenge.

The professor went ashore. Standing in the middle of the stone circle, he checked the position of the Pole Star and noted that it showed the structure was aligned north-south. Because this monument was prehistoric and was built in the days when the Pole Star's constellation had not reached its present position in the sky, Professor Thom deduced that the people who had built it must have had some other way of determining the alignment of the stones.

His discovery there launched him on a quest around 600 standing stone sites both in Britain and Europe. It proved that although the stone circles may look rough and weathered today, worn down by both time and human activities, they were originally precise works of engineering skill. Of Stonehenge, he declared that it was a Stone Age observatory, where even small irregularities on the extremities of the site were created artificially, specifically to mark the significant moments when the sun and moon rose and set.

In 1963 Gerald Hawkins, Professor of Astronomy at Boston University, made another startling claim. He stated that Stonehenge was like a giant computer: a huge observatory capable of extremely complex calculations based on the position of the sun, moon and stars. When Hawkins fed all the data he had about the site into a computer, the startling result was that the stones could be used to predict the occurrence of eclipses. Why not accept such sophistication among the ancients, he argued to the critics, since the men who built it had proved by the feat itself that they were not primitive?

Hawkins' observatory theory gained ground, thanks to the work of C.A. Newham, who said the highly educated astronomer priests of the time could have stood in the centre of the great circle and determined the position of the sun or moon in its orbit by using the stones as a guide.

More dramatically, in 1976 Dr Euan Mackie of Glasgow's Hunterian Museum announced that he had found the site of the elite academy where these gifted priests may have lived and studied their craft. He said that remains found at Durrington Walls, near Stonehenge, showed a race of people who ate a rich diet, who wore woven cloth and who enjoyed a status above that of their nearest neighbours.

Professor Sir Fred Hoyle, one of Britain's most famous astronomers, supported the theory that Stonehenge was a giant observatory. Hoyle agreed that the megaliths could be used as markers to gauge the moon's activity as it passed through different stages of its cycle. He added that Stonehenge's construction 'demanded a level of intellectual attainment higher than the standard to be expected from a community of primitive farmers.'

If the academics are right, that Stonehenge and the other standing stone sites were designed for making astronomical observations, it is likely that there was an intellectual elite within the primitive Stone Age farmers we know inhabited the earth – an elite who carried out the complex calculations necessary to chart planetary movements in an age when there was no written word.

Other theories about Stonehenge exist . . . that the site was a beacon for aliens from outer space, a temple for human sacrifice, even that it was a place where infertile women went to be blessed by ancient gods. But the observatory theory stands best the test of time. Scientists now accept the once unbelievable proposition that a phenomenally intellectual race long ago learned to operate a gigantic stone 'computer'!

The Great Pyramid

Of all the ancient world's Seven Wonders, just one survives. It stands as testimony to human genius, constructed 45 centuries ago to house the remains of a ruler judged by his people to be both mortal and divine. It covers an area of 5.25 hectares, took 30 years to construct and is made from enough stone to build a wall all the way around Cairo, the nearest city. It is the Great Pyramid of Cheops.

The magnificent structure is the largest of three at Giza, outside Cairo. The colour of burnt ochre against a brilliant blue sky, it was built by an army of labourers, probably numbering in excess of 20,000 for the Pharaoh Cheops, successor to Seneferu, who died around 2520 BC.

Little is known of the great Cheops, except that he started preparations for his afterlife while still a young man. It was his ambition to be interred in the greatest pyramid of all, surrounded by great treasures.

Egyptian kings considered themselves living gods, destined to leave earth to travel with the other deities, particularly the Sun God, Ra, and to voyage with him in his 'boat of a million years' — by day through the skies, and by night through the dark and treacherous underworld.

The first pyramids were step-shaped in design, literally providing a walkway to the sky. But in Cheops' reign (Cheops is the Greek name given to him, the Egyptian one being Khufu) the golden age of pyramid building dawned and the greatest structures were made. They are feats of engineering that make modern-day architects and engineers gasp in awe at the astonishing accuracy of their construction.

The ancient Egyptians knew no metals other then copper and gold, so most tools for shaping and chipping stone were made from flint and wood. Wood was used, too, to hammer into faults in quarry stone. The wood was then soaked and, when it swelled, it split the stone into huge chunks, some weighing up to fifteen tons. The stones were then hauled into place on wet rollers by teams of men.

The architects had to be certain of a flat surface for the site of the Great Pyramid. However, they had no means, such as modern-day spirit levels, of ascertaining where that might be. So in a long, laborious process, they dug canals, flooded an area and, knowing that where the water lay along the surface was flat land, chose their site. The land was then drained and construction could begin.

It is still staggering to think that mortals, even armed with that small knowledge, should have

The Great Pyramid of Cheops at Giza. The manpower required to construct this amazing structure – 20,000 slaves working for 30 years.

built a pyramid 147 metres high, covering a base 230 metres along each side and weighing in excess of 6 million tons. The lengths of the longest and shortest sides differ by just 20 centimetres, and, incredibly, the pavement around the Great Pyramid is level to within 2.5 centimetres. Although these masters of civilisation chronicled so many things all those years ago, the Egyptians left no records to help us with this puzzle. When the first archaeologists studied the monumental structure, they found it was impossible to slide a needle between the great limestone, granite and sandstone blocks.

Mystics point out that the pyramid's walls run exactly from North to South and East to West, and believe that the ancient Egyptians used the star Alpha Draconis, nearest to the north celestial pole, to achieve this precise orientation.

The only entrance to the tomb is on the north side of the pyramid, and in case of the king's sudden death while work was still in progress, the pyramid was made with three tombs inside. The first was deep in the underlying rock, the second in the heart of the pyramid, and the final burial chamber 42 metres up. A great gallery, 47.5 metres long and 7.9 metres wide, was created to allow access to the burial chamber. However, the gallery itself could be reached only by walking bent double through narrow corridors.

Some of the earliest Western eyes to gaze on the Cheops Pyramid did so when Napoleon, on one of his wars of conquest, went to war with the Egyptians. Napoleon was spellbound by the magnificence of the pyramids, and together with his army brought out scholars and scientists to chronicle, decipher and plunder this cornucopia of ancient wonders.

Napoleon instilled in his men the sense of awe they should feel when in the presence of such a structure. Before clashing with the forces of the Turkish emperor, outside the gates of Cairo in 1798, Napoleon exhorted his troops: 'Remember that from the top of these monuments, 40 centuries are looking down on you.'

The world owes the French scholars in Napoleon's ranks a great deal, for they unravelled the mysteries of hieroglyphics and the ancient Coptic scripts, and charted the great historical sites. But no one in nineteenth century Europe could fathom why the pyramids had been built.

Although the Great Pyramid is a work of technical brilliance, Egyptologists are still puzzled as to whether King Cheops was actually laid to rest in it. Certainly, it remained undisturbed for 3000 years until an Arab, Abdullah al Mamun, and his band of men discovered in AD 820 a passageway to the inside. Finding it blocked by huge granite boulders, they forced their way round into the King's Chamber – only to find his granite sarcophagus empty.

Did the priests ever inter him there? Or was, as many believe, the Great Pyramid constructed for more mysterious, secret reasons?

In 1864 Charles Piazzi Smyth, Astronomer Royal for Scotland, visited the site of the Great Pyramid and began work on a new theory. Ten years later he published a best selling work entitled *Our Inheritance in the Great Pyramid*. In the work Smyth concocted a fascinating, if not at times a little far-fetched, reason for the construction of the pyramid.

It was, he argued, a gigantic touchstone, a desert fortune-teller which, if all its measurements both inside and out were taken, had enormous religious and scientific value. The pyramid's measurements, when decoded, Smyth argued, foretold the history of man right up to the Second Coming of Christ. Smyth called his new theory 'pyramidology'.

One who was determined to debunk Smyth's theory of the Great Pyramid was the man destined to become the greatest Egyptologist of the all, the British archaeologist William Flinders Petrie. Petrie arrived at Giza in 1880 and began a methodical scientific survey, abandoning the preconceptions of the 'hogwash' (as he termed it) ideas of pyramidology.

In 1883 he published *Pyramids and Temples of Giza*, largely demolishing the myth that messages and mysteries were encoded in the great blocks of stone. Instead he took them for what they were – astonishing feats of engineering and design, replete with false passages and dead ends, boulders and sealed rooms to ward off tomb robbers. This was not, he declared, the creation of a great force, a mysterious and unknown being; it was simply the work of a gifted race which sought to ennoble its dead in man-made mountains for all eternity.

Even so, Petrie, who went on to study all the pyramids of Egypt and their origins, has not destroyed the belief of the many who say that, because of the way they are constructed, pyramids do exert a strange life-force – and that within them, strange things can happen.

Whichever theory you choose to subscribe to, everyone agrees on one thing: nothing like them has ever been built, nor has anything like them endured so long. And, save for the highly polished limestone-slab covering which would have been a metre thick, running from the apex to base of the pyramid on all four sides, the Great Pyramid of Cheops is the same as the one gazed upon by the great pharaoh himself.

Atlantis

It is the essential stuff of legend. According to stories retold over the centuries, a people of great wealth, beauty and happiness inhabited an island called Atlantis. This paradise was blessed with lush vegetation, a cultured and civilised populace, a wealth of natural minerals including gold and silver, and food in abundance.

But did Atlantis really ever exist? If so, where was it – and what was the catastrophe that destroyed it?

Few great unanswered mysteries can have had as much energy, thought and words expended on them as that surrounding the legendary lost city. Some 2000 books (a conservative estimate) have been written about Atlantis, most of them hinging on the single most perplexing question of the whole story: where was it?

The source of legends about the great city of Atlantis was, of course, the first author ever to write about it: Plato. The great Greek philosopher wrote an account in 347 BC of a kingdom which vanished from the face of the earth centuries before the birth of Christ. He told how, as a young man, he listened to Socrates discussing philosophy with a group of students including his friend Critias. Together the assembled group talked of Atlantis, a kingdom 'derived from historical tradition'.

It was described as a once-great nation, whose people became corrupt and whose leaders led it into decline. According to the Egyptian priests quoted by Critias, Atlantis was destroyed by a violent volcanic eruption, which was followed by a tidal wave that plunged the tragic island beneath the waves forever.

Since then, and thanks to Plato's account, Atlantis has become a holy grail for many adventurers, archaeologists, historians and others fascinated with legends. But not one of them has been able to find the submerged remains of the ancient utopia.

Plato puts the date for the destruction of Atlantis at some time around 9600 BC, the location being 'beyond the Pillars of Hercules' (or Straits of Gibraltar). He describes the magical land thus:

'At the centre of the island, near the sea, was a plain, said to be the most beautiful and fertile of all plains, and near the middle of this plain . . . a hill of no great size. In the centre was a shrine sacred to Poseidon and Cleito, surrounded by a golden wall through which entry was forbidden.'

He goes on to describe the magnificent hot and cold springs, the elaborate temples, and the luxurious accommodation afforded to visiting royalty. In all, he paints a splendid picture of a kingdom which enjoyed, before its decline and fall, the greatest benefits of civilisation.

Since Plato's day, Atlantis has been 'placed' in every sea and ocean — from the Sargasso to the Scilly Isles, from the Pacific to the centre of the Atlantic. Authors have envisaged a once-massive land bridge between Britain and America via Iceland and Greenland.

Perhaps the most credible possible site is that of Bimini, a small island in the Bahamas which, although its likelihood of being a place of great historical importance is small, has a gigantic question mark hanging over it as the result of a series of unexplained finds. In 1969 a fisherman known as Bonefish Sam brought archaeologist Dr J. Manson Valentine to view curious rectangular stones lying in 25 feet of water north of a spot called Paradise Point. Manson Valentine was ecstatic, believing the two parallel lines of stones, about a quarter of a mile long and 15 feet square, to be the remnants of a great harbour wall.

Hordes of archaeologists immediately descended on sleepy Bimini to investigate whether the stones were the work of Aztec, Toltec, Mayan or other civilisations. No one has been able to prove their origins either way. However, two later expeditions to Bimini in 1975 and 1977 revealed a block of stone with a carved edge, something definitely crafted by man. To this date, its origin has not been established.

Although the Atlantis described by Plato has never been found, there are academics who subscribe to the notion that the philosopher mistook the location of Atlantis and that the catastrophe referred to was the mighty volcanic eruption which blasted the Minoan civilisation off the face of the earth.

Derek Ager, head of the Department of Geology at Bristol University, says: 'I have no doubt at all that there never was such a land mass beyond the Pillars of Hercules. The subject is just not worth discussing. On the other hand, I think it is quite possible, even probable, that the legend refers to the destruction of the Minoan civilisation by the volcanic process.'

So was the Atlantis described by Plato the Bronze Age Minoan culture which blossomed in the islands of the Aegean until around 1500 BC? There is a great deal of evidence that suggests it may have been.

The Minoans ruled from their magnificent city of Knossos, on the island of Crete. From here, the Minoan people dominated the Aegean Sea and the hundreds of islands in it. What became of this mighty civilisation in its dying days is now lost in time; or at least it was until 1967, when a Greek archaeologist, Spyridon Marinatos, began excavating on one of those isles, the southern-most of the Cyclades islands.

Marinatos project was to delve into the history of the island of Kalliste, as it was then called in ancient times, although it is now known as Santorini or Thera. There, buried beneath 100 feet of volcanic ash, he discovered the remains of a city whose people were civilised and refined. They enjoyed mains drainage and baths in their homes, unrivalled prosperity and command of the seas.

Then suddenly their golden civilisation was destroyed by volcanic blasts of such magnitude as to defy belief. Scientists believe the eruptions were four times greater than that which destroyed the Indonesian isle of Krakatoa in 1883, producing the loudest bang in recorded history. His find became known as the 'Pompeii of the Aegean' after the famous Roman town that was also destroyed by a volcano.

Archaeologists believe that when minor earthquakes and eruptions alerted the Minoans to the danger they were in, the population took to the sea in boats. They were probably no more than 150 miles away, however, when the main eruptions occurred – raining down burning debris and choking ash on their vessels before tidal waves made matchsticks of the ones which escaped the firestorm.

The ash clouds which followed the eruptions are even believed by some historians to be the origin of the story of the Egyptian plagues described in the Old Testament. Certainly, the pall that hung over Kalliste would have been visible as far away as Egypt.

So did the cultured Minoans become the fabled Atlanteans of Plato's story? For 500 years they ruled supreme and then they vanished. Archaeology tells us that Kalliste may be the site of Atlantis – and that Plato may not merely have been reciting a legend.

Teotihuacan

As Europe sank into a barbarous, dark age, there existed far across the oceans a civilisation that today we can only marvel at. Its principal city was Teotihuacan – and it was one of the most spectacular of the ancient world.

At a time when barbarian hordes were destroying the cities of Europe and the remnants of the mighty Roman empire had crumbled, this civilisation on the plains of Mexico achieved a level of culture and sophistication that puzzles and intrigues historians and archaeologists to this day. We know its inhabitants were literate, numerate and were deeply religious, but we have no idea who this race of cultured people was.

The builders of the city of Teotihuacan (a name given to it by those who populated it long after its founders had gone) displayed a skill almost as great as that deployed by the pyramid builders of ancient Egypt, and evolved a society as cultured as any of the ancient world. While the old European world burned under the torches of the Huns, Goths and Vandals, the educated citizens of this gracious city, with its pyramids and wide avenues, feasted on the finest produce, crafted beautiful pottery and stoneware and learned to count and to read.

What is baffling about Teotihuacan, situated near the sprawling, modern capital Mexico City, is the lack of clues as to the identity of the race which created it – and why it seemingly abandoned the city, like some landlocked Mary Celeste, and vanished from the face of the earth.

The ancient remains, which attract thousands of visitors each year, are part of a city which once stretched over 23 square kilometres and give the feeling that a race of people, numbering some 200,000, lived a good life in a well-ordered, well-structured society.

The city stands on a plateau 2,250 metres above sea level at a place where several important routes converge. The surrounding land is good for the cultivation of maize, tomatoes, beans, avocados and pumpkins. The city itself was laid out in precisely patterned streets, dominated by two pyramids, replete with ornately decorated temples and palaces.

When that other great Mexican civilisation, the Aztecs, stumbled upon the ruins of the city 1000 years after it reached its zenith, they bestowed upon it their own name, Teotihuacan: 'the place of those who have the road of the gods'. The Aztecs, like modern-day historians, were puzzled as to the origins of the people who built this great metropolis.

Archaeologists think that nine-tenths of

Teotihuacan lies buried under the dust from the surrounding plains that has settled over the area through the years. It is generally thought to have been constructed in the first century AD, and during the eight hundred or so years of security and prosperity it enjoyed, its people engaged in regular building and restructuring work.

Archaeological exploration has unearthed several layers of the city. The Pyramid of the Sun is the dominating central feature of the city, standing beside the Avenue of the Dead, the main thoroughfare. Experts calculate that the pyramid would have taken 3000 men no less than 30 years to build.

Its axis is aligned east-west, reflecting the path of the sun across the sky. It is generally thought that the pyramid was built to represent the universe, with its four corners symbolising the points of the compass, with its apex representing the 'heart of life'. Each side of the pyramid measures 225 metres and is 70 metres high, with a total mass of some two-and-a-half million tons of dried brick and rubble.

Its sister pyramid, smaller in size, is the Pyramid of the Moon, 43 metres high, standing at the northern end of the Avenue of the Dead. Directly in front of this pyramid is the plaza of the Moon, which leads to the Citadel, the religious heart of the metropolis, where stands the Temple of Quetzalcoatl: the 'feathered serpent' god. The Avenue of the Dead contained the houses of the city's elite – the priests, minor functionaries and the leaders themselves – while the remainder of the population lived in the surrounding area.

At the height of its power, the city walls shone with brilliant frescoes of gods and men, emblazoned in beautiful, striking colours, while the temples were adorned with black basalt and elaborately stuccoed. Relics have been found which testify to the artistic genius of the populace, in such items as a tripod vase, pots, graceful eating bowls and numerous figures.

The inhabitants invented a system of writing (which has still to be properly decoded and understood) and a system of numeracy based on dots and bars. But who were they?

Research has shown that before Teotihuacan was built, Indians lived in and around the fertile plain in primitive wattle-and-daub huts, probably in clusters of no more than 300 people. Some greater, more intelligent tribe or race harnessed the labour force already in existence in their primitive homes to construct the city with its road to the gods.

Various theories have been put forward as to who they were. A Frenchman Desire Charnay, who stumbled upon the site in 1880, believed it to be an ancient Toltec ruin. But it is generally held that the Toltec race arrived after Teotihuacan was in ruins, and its splendour decayed.

Mexican scholar Jimenez Moreno believes that Teotihuacan was ruled by a priestly autocracy because of the prominence of buildings of religious significance. He points to the celestial significance of the Pyramids of the Sun and Moon, and argues that the whole purpose of the city was the worship of the gods who had apparently blessed the surrounding region with agricultural and wildlife stocks in plenty.

The fact remains, though, that there is no real clue as to who this master race was. Certainly it was a religious race, as evidenced by the Temple of Quetzalcoatl, the god who represented the union of heaven and earth, land and water.

The French archaeological expert, Laurette Sejourne, argues that the whole city may have been built to Quetzalcoatl's glory, with the buildings around the temple reserved for priests. In those buildings they would have been initiated into the ancient rites before ascending the steps of the Pyramid of the Sun for a final ceremony that would mark them as fully fledged servants of their deity.

It is safe to speculate that religion did indeed play a major part in the life the people of Teotihuacan, shown not only by the name which the Aztecs were later to bestow on the city, but also by the countless religious artefacts that are slowly being unearthed from the site. But it was also more than just a giant place of worship; it was a busy, thriving city which positively hummed with activity.

There is as marvellous tableau showing market day in Teotihuacan which has been put on display in the Museum of Natural History in Mexico City. It vividly depicts thousands of peasants bartering meats, fowl, fish, vegetables and other goods just as in a modern-day street market.

The remains of vegetable and animal matter found in the cooking pots and refuse pits of ruined houses have indicated that the inhabitants enjoyed a healthy diet. The housing complexes were lavish or simple, depending on whether nobles, priests or commoners inhabited them. One palace, called Zacuala, covered an area of over 3300 square metres and boasted its own private temple. Courtyard complexes which have recently been discovered showed that rainwater was carried away in an elaborate drainage system, which could be plugged if water supplies were getting low.

Remains have been found beneath the houses. It seems that the citizens treated their dead with great reverence. After the bodies of loved ones were cremated, the ashes were blessed by the high priests before being wrapped in linen shrouds and buried beneath the homes of their families. Apart from ashes, skeletons have been unearthed, buried with ritual offerings of pottery. Indeed, some of the most well preserved pottery of the highest artistic quality found at Teotihuacan has been discovered in the burial sites, denoting the importance of a dignified death ceremony which the inhabitants valued.

Professor Rene Millon, of the University of New York at Rochester, has devoted much of his life to the study of Teotihuacan. He thinks that by the year AD 150 there was a population of over 50,000 – many of them the former hut dwellers who abandoned their primitive abodes for the safety and culture of the city. Professor Millon charts the growth of the city – at its height it was bigger than Caesar's Rome – until it reached its peak in about the fifth and sixth centuries.

Teotihuacan fell into decline in about the middle of the sixth century AD, the inhabitants finally leaving the city around the eighth century. But why that decline occurred is as baffling a mystery as the foundation of the city itself . . .

There have been found none of the traces of pillage and bloodshed associated with cities that fall by the sword. Nor have there been indications that the citizens left in a blind panic, or were wiped out by plague or famine.

The theory has been put forward that the populace rebelled against the priest-rulers because of the ever-growing numbers of human sacrifices offered to the gods in harsh years. But there is little, if any, evidence that the people of Teotihuacan practised human sacrifice; and if they did, it was accepted practice in the majority of Central American cultures before the spread of Christianity. Some evidence of fires has been unearthed among the ruins. These may have been started deliberately, but it hardly seems likely that the people would have used this method to try to destroy a stone city. It is more likely that the race which followed and moved into the city put the artefacts of their predecessors to the torch.

Archaeologists continue to argue about the decline and fall of Teotihuacan. Did a marauding tribe sweep down from the north, driving civilian populations before them? Did the population rebel against the priesthood, corrupt in its power, or simply leave in a mass exodus? There are no answers to these questions, and the city of the gods stands as an enigma which will continue to defy explanation for centuries to come.

The New World

Christopher Columbus is credited with being the first European to set foot in America. But did he open up the New World to the Old? Or did the Chinese, Phoenician, Irish, Viking or Ancient Greek sailors get there first?

Undoubtedly, Columbus was the supreme voyager of his age. The brave, pioneering sailor is universally celebrated as the discoverer of America in 1492 when he sailed from Spain to the West Indies. But was he? Researchers suggest that many other races, equipped with vessels far more primitive than his, could have reached it before him. Thor Heyerdahl, the Norwegian ethnologist, showed that the ancient Egyptians could have reached America long before Columbus, when, in 1967, he crossed the Atlantic in a boat made of papyrus.

Indeed, scientists can prove that man has been settled in America for 12,000 years – a fact ascertained using the process of carbon dating, which accurately reads the amount of radioactivity in materials and is capable of pinpointing their date to within a hundred years. These first settlers were the descendants of Mongolian tribesmen who had reached the continent by crossing the land bridge across the Bering Straits from Siberia to Alaska.

This much we know of the indigenous people, the first Americans. But who were the first people from other continents to reach America?

Could, for instance, the Chinese, masters of the seas long before European traders, have been the first outsiders to land in America? Sculptures found amongst the remains of ancient Central American nations have had such an uncanny resemblance to idols used in Buddhist religion that some theorists claim the Chinese arrived there in about 2000 BC.

One eminent academic, Professor Chu Shienchi of Beijing University, believes a Buddhist priest named Hoei Shin voyaged across the Pacific Ocean and landed on the coastline of the Gulf of Mexico. He claims that documentary evidence in China shows that Hoei Shin named the site of his discovery Fusang, after a Chinese plant which he said was similar to flora growing there.

Another race which may have set foot in America before the time of Christ were the Phoenicians. In 600 BC the Ancient Greek historian Herodotus wrote of the Phoenicians when he told of sailors from Tyre and Sidon being hired by Pharaoh Necho of Egypt to sail around Africa and out across the Atlantic in oared galleys. If they did not reach the New World, they

The *Ra*, the remarkable boat built by the Norwegian Thor Heyerdahl. Heyerdahl sailed the boat from Morocco to Barbados in 1969 –

showing that the ancient Egyptians could have reached America before Columbus.

almost certainly reached the Azores, where a hoard of gold Carthaginian coins were discovered only in the eighteenth century.

But it was the discovery in South America of an inscribed stone which pro-Phoenician theorists hold up as proof of their claims. The stone was found in a Brazilian coffee plantation in 1872. Since then its script has been examined by many eminent academics. Some say it is counterfeit; others, like Cyrus Gordon, Professor of Ancient History from Brandeis University, Massachusetts, have declared it original. The translation reads:

'We are sons of Canaan from Sidon, the city of the King. Commerce has cast us in this distant shore, a land of mountains. We set [the word for human sacrifice] a youth for the exalted gods and goddesses in the eighteenth year of Hiram, our mighty King. We embarked from Ezion-Geber into the Red Sea and voyaged with ten ships. We were at sea together for two years around the land belonging to Ham [Africa]. But we were separated by a storm and we were no longer with our companions. So we have come here, twelve men and three women on a new shore which I, the Admiral, control. But auspiciously may the exalted gods and goddesses favour us.'

Is this conclusive proof that they were there long before the birth of Christ? The Phoenicians may have been the greatest navigators of their age, but the scant historical evidence makes it difficult to substantiate claims that they were the first to reach America. The argument rages on to this day.

Another claim for historical eminence is made for the ancient Celts. The evidence for such a claim lies on desolate Mystery Hill in North Salem, north of Boston, where lie a collection of ruins of a kind more usually associated with the great megalithic sites of Europe. There are the remains of 22 huts, passageways and cooking pits, and an eerie sacrificial table with a speaking tube through which voices can be projected – presumably for use during macabre ceremonies.

The huge blocks of granite comprising the passageways are held in place by their own weight, and many thousands of artefacts from different periods have been uncovered there. Stones bearing chiselled inscriptions in the ancient Celtic form of rune writing called Ogam have also been found.

The Celtic claim is, of course, often argued about and oft disputed. However, there is little dispute over the fact that Viking adventurers voyaged to North America in their longboats centuries before Columbus.

The discovery of eight houses, cooking pots, kitchen implements, boats and boat sheds at a site on the northern tip of Newfoundland offer, says

Norwegian historian Dr Helge Ingstad, 'the first incontrovertible evidence that Europeans set foot in America centuries before Columbus's voyage of 1492'.

The Vikings travelled in short stages from Scandinavia, via Iceland and Greenland, establishing settlements en route. They were well supplied, developing a method of preserving their meats by trailing them in the salted water, and drinking water from cowhide pouches.

An ancient saga recounting the deeds of the great navigator Leif Ericsson recounts that he reached the New World in the year 1000 AD and called it Vinland. It was, he recorded, a land of beauty and contrasting climates. The great navigator was probably referring to the region now known as New England.

Evidence that the Norsemen trod further inland than even New England arose in 1898 when a farmer clearing land at Kensington, Minnesota, uncovered a large stone inscribed with the characters of a strange language. The Kensington Rune, as it became known, retold the story of a 30-strong party of Norwegians and Goths who went west from Vinland in 1362, ending with a massacre in which ten of the party were killed.

The authenticity of the Kensington Rune has been disputed. So has that of another ruin which seemed to offer positive proof of the Vikings' first foothold on the continent. The Newport Tower, in Rhode Island, is a circular structure supported on eight columns and is reckoned to be old enough to have been constructed by the Vikings. Others, however, claim that the building is merely the remains of a church built by much later, Christian settlers.

Leif Ericsson's account of his adventures in the ancient Norse sagas are often fanciful, as is to be expected. But there is little dramatisation in their telling and, it seems, no boasting about their undoubted prowess. For the great Norse sailors testify in their sagas that it was not they but the Irish who were the first to reach America!

For further proof of this claim we must look to another ancient document: a sixth century Latin manuscript, the *Navigatio Sancti Brendani*, which is often quoted as evidence for the Irish being the first Europeans to cross the Atlantic. The *Navigatio*, which has survived to the present day, tells how St. Brendan, an experienced sailor from Kerry in the west of Ireland, and fourteen monks set sail in 540 AD 'to find the land promised to the saints'.

Their craft, a 35 foot ketch covered with the hides of oxen and waterproofed with butter, must have taken a northerly course. For the *Navigatio* talks of their encountering 'a floating tower of crystal' – probably an iceberg. St Brendan's expedition then passed through an area of dense mist – possibly the famous fog-shrouded Newfoundland Banks. Eventually they landed on a lushly vegetated island surrounded by clear waters and inhabited by pygmies. A final voyage took them on to a semi-tropical mainland.

The story is far from unbelievable. The island could have been one of the Bahamian chain. And the land they later found could have been Florida.

Apart from the Irish, Vikings and Phoenicians, there are many other contenders for the honour of being the first outsiders to discover America. But in every case, the evidence falls tantalisingly short of being proof.

Perhaps until that proof is obtained, Christopher Columbus, the Italian adventurer employed by a Spanish king, should be allowed to keep his place in the history books. The only tragedy is that, when he set foot in the New World, he did not realise where he had landed. When poor Columbus died on 20 May 1506, he still did not know that the land he had stumbled upon was in fact the vast continent of America.

El Dorado

El Dorado! It's a name that has gone down in the varied languages of the world as a by-word for fabled wealth. It conjures up visions of idyllic landscapes and a flourishing culture. The legend has tantalised the inquisitive and tempted the greedy. And it has often been difficult to decide which has been the greater lure to mortal mankind: the search for El Dorado's lost civilisation or the search for its ancient gold.

The Old World first heard of El Dorado when the Spanish conquistadors, under the ruthless Francisco Pizarro, invaded the Incas in 1530, captured their capital city of Cuzco, and plundered their golden art treasures. After a terrible reign of looting and pillaging, in which the Spanish stripped the entire Inca empire of its age-old wealth, the conquistadors began to look further afield for even greater treasure chests.

The dream of a fresh fortune beyond the Inca empire was fuelled by extraordinary myths and legends. Sebastian de Belalcazar, who founded the Ecuador capital of Quito, heard the stories and coined the name El Dorado. But he failed to find the place. The Spanish believed that El Dorado was a secret Inca city surrounded by a land of treasure-filled temples waiting to be plundered.

Between 1535 and 1540 several expeditions led by different foreign powers sought the lost city supposedly lying to the north of known Inca territory. One was led by Georg Hohermuth, German governor of Venezuela, who, with 400 men, searched for 3 years for the city. His expedition suffered starvation and sickness and returned empty handed, leaving 300 of his expedition dead in the jungle. Yet unbeknown to him, he had passed just 60 miles from El Dorado!

The largest expedition ever assembled was led by the brutal Spaniard, Gonzalo Jimenez de Quesada, in 1536. Disease and battles with the Chibcha Indians of Colombia reduced his mercenary army from 900 to 200. But Quesada succeeded in capturing villages, where the tortured inhabitants were forced to reveal their treasures of precious metals and gems.

Quesada was led by captive Indians to the town of Hunsa, described as the 'place of gold'. There they found a chieftain's house the walls of which were lined with massive sheets of beaten gold. The chief sat on a beautiful throne of gold and emeralds. His temples were stacked with gold plates and large hoards of emeralds and bags of gold dust. The Spaniards made a pact with the Indians – then slaughtered every one of them, even stealing the gold rings from the ears and noses of the corpses.

It was here in the blood-drenched streets of Indian jungle towns that the legend of El Dorado became not just a mystery but an enigma for all time – the natives told Quesada that El Dorado was not a place but a person.

El Dorado is Spanish for 'The Gilded One'. The Indians interpreted this as meaning the chieftain of the Muisca nation, who lived in the region in which now sits the Colombian capital of Bogota. The remnants of Quesada's expedition were led to Lake Guatavita, 9000 feet above sea level, where the chiefs of the Muiscas were once crowned in a unique ritual.

The chief's tribe would gather around the perfectly circular lake while the new chief, stripped naked and his body coated in gold dust, set sail for the centre. With the sun glinting on his body, the king would then make his offerings to the gods by dropping gold treasures into the deep waters of Lake Guatavita. His subjects would then follow his lead by hurling their golden offerings from the shore.

El Dorado, however, remained as elusive to the Spaniards as the sunset on the waters of Lake Guatavita. For the last Muisca chief to be enthroned on the lake had been deposed a few years earlier; and El Dorado's people had sought no new gold since they no longer needed it for the glittering but defunct coronation ceremonies.

Over the years, the Indians' greedy tormentors sent expedition after expedition to attempt to plumb the lake's depths. Members of Quesada's original team returned in 1545 to conscript the Muisca Indians into a human chain from the water's edge to the mountain top. Bucketful by bucketful, for three months they took water from the lake and passed it along the line to be tipped away. The level dropped by only 9 feet and several hundred gold artefacts recovered before the emptying of the lake was finally abandoned.

In 1585 another Spanish expedition recruited 8000 Indians to cut a deep channel to drain the lake. This time the level fell by 60 feet and many more golden objects were uncovered before landslides blocked the drainage channel.

The last serious attempt to drain the lake was undertaken by British fortune seekers at the beginning of this century. They drilled a tunnel which lowered the water level, but again the drainage channels silted up.

The Colombian government has long since passed laws protecting the lake from treasure-hunters. However, it is beyond reason to think that the poor Muisca Indians threw every ounce of their precious treasures into the depths all those centuries ago.

The Man in the Iron Mask

Who was the Man in the Iron Mask? Why, for 30 years, was he forced to wear the infernal contraption? He ate with it on, slept with it on, and had his teeth inspected through it by doctors as though it were little more than a special brace. Even in death, the grotesque apparatus stayed on his face.

The jaw-piece of the mask was flanged with special springs to allow movement for speech and chewing, but the side panels which bonded the apparatus together were riveted firmly to foil any attempt at removal. The unfortunate man doomed to wear this for over three decades was threatened with instant death if he ever breathed a word of his true identity, or mentioned the reason for his strange incarceration.

When this poor wretch finally died in one of the countless cells of France's most infamous jail, the Bastille, in 1703, his clothes were flung into a furnace, the ironwork in his cell was melted down and the scant furniture was burned. Even the whitewash was removed in case he had tried to leave a pitiful message revealing his true self.

It was as if he had never existed. The stories about him, however, have survived the centuries. So has the enigma of his identity.

Later immortalised by the novelist Alexander Dumas, the Man in the Iron Mask was kept prisoner by Louis XIV, the Sun King. It was on the direct orders of the extravagant ruler who built the magnificent Palace of Versailles that the prisoner's identity was kept a secret.

Yet, although his crime must have been heinous indeed to warrant the attention of the monarch (though seemingly not serious enough to incur execution), the wretched captive was permitted certain privileges. He was allowed to attend mass without hindrance, was given books and fine food and allowed luxuries not normally granted to prisoners in the Bastille.

Rumours of the celebrated convict abounded in France before the Revolution. None of the correspondence between prison officials and court functionaries known at that time ever referred to his real identity but there were some fantastic theories about who he really was.

According to one, he was the twin brother of Louis XIV, and was locked away by the monarch because, in his vanity, he wished to preserve all the glory and privilege of the throne for himself.

According to another theory, he was an illegitimate son of the king, conceived after a secret liaison with a farm girl. It was said that his appearance so closely matched the king's that he could never be allowed to be seen in public.

It was not until the Man in the Iron Mask died that gossip and public intrigue began to chip away at the wall of secrecy which surrounded this mysterious figure.

In 1753, a full 50 years after his ignoble end in the Bastille, a private journal of Etienne du Jonca, the king's lieutenant in the jail at the time of his imprisonment, came to light – and it mentioned the strange, masked prisoner.

It announced his arrival at the Bastille in 1698, when he had already spent nearly 30 years behind bars at other prisons – always in the custody of the same governor: the only man, it was later learned, who was ever allowed to see him unmasked. The journal read:

'Thursday 18 September at three o'clock, M de Saint-Mars, Governor of the Chateau of the Bastille, made his appearance, coming from the command of the Iles-Sainte-Marguerite-Pignerol, whom he caused always to be masked, whose name is not mentioned.'

Five years after that entry, du Jonca recorded the death of the 'unknown prisoner' and testified to the use of a black velvet mask. However, many historians believe this may have been merely a belated stab at decency by the authorities, who could have removed the iron contraption from his body shortly after his death and fitted a loose cloth one in its place.

Du Jonca also recorded that the prisoner was buried at the Bastille under the false name of Marchioly. The name led to another wild rumour about him: that he was a man named Mattioli, an envoy of the Duke of Mantua, who had once incurred the displeasure of the king. This theory was later disproved. Mattioli certainly existed, and was even imprisoned in Pignerol, in the same tower as the mystery man. But his penal servitude was widely publicised as a warning that no man crossed the king of France and got away with it.

Few other descriptions of the captive exist, but one which has survived demonstrates the lengths to which the authorities were prepared to go to preserve the secret of his true identity. When de Saint-Mars was bringing his important prisoner from St Marguerite in the Bay of Cannes up to the Bastille in Paris, they stopped to dine at de Saint-Mars' chateau near Villeneuve. Peasants who glanced through the windows of the chateau as they ate noticed that next to de Saint-Mars' plates were loaded pistols, ready to be aimed at his charge should he attempt to reveal his face to the domestic staff.

De Saint-Mars was privileged indeed to have been entrusted with the secret of the identity of the Man in the Iron Mask. For even within the House of Bourbon, only Louis XV came to know the secret. He is alleged to have said, on hearing who the man was: 'If he were still alive, I would give him his freedom.'

The information was never confided to Louis XVI, who began a fruitless search to discover it, largely to satisfy the curiosity of his truculent and eccentric wife, Marie Antoinette.

It was only with the overthrow of the monarchy in the French Revolution in 1789 that the first real clues as to the man's true identity began to emerge. When state files were plundered, it came to light in the records of the Minister of War, a man called Louvois, that a large number of letters had passed between him and de Saint-Mars concerning the mystery man. At the end of July 1669, the year in which the Man in the Iron Mask was first imprisoned, Louvois wrote in a letter to the prison governor:

'The king has commanded that I am to have the man named Eustache Dauger sent to Pignerol. It is of the utmost importance to his service that he should be most securely guarded at all times and that he should in no way give information about himself nor send letters to anyone at all. You will yourself once a day have to take enough food for the day to this wretch and you must on no account listen for any reason at all to what he may want to say to you, always threatening to kill him if he opens his mouth to speak of anything but his necessities.'

Another letter, from the king himself to de Saint-Mars, survived in the archives, and reads:

'I am sending to my citadel of Pignerol, in the charge of Captain de Vauroy, sergeant major of my city and citadel of Dunkirk, the man named Eustache Dauger. You are to hold him in good and safe custody, preventing him from communicating with anyone at all by word of mouth or writ of hand.'

Could it be that Eustache Dauger was the Man in the Iron Mask?

If he was, how could he possibly be so dangerous to the king of France that he was locked away, forced to suffer the unbearable indignity of having his face encased in iron and was forbidden to communicate his identity on pain of death?

Later research has proved that Eustache Dauger came from a large family and had five sisters and six brothers, four of whom were killed in battle, and was a native of the northern French port of Dunkirk. But why the incarceration?

Some historians believe that Dauger's one surviving brother was made a marquis, enabling Dauger to mingle with the nobility. He may have been introduced to Louis XIV at court. At the age of 22, while serving as a lieutenant in the King's Guards, he was caught celebrating a black mass – a blasphemous travesty of the Christian Mass. It is also widely believed that the person with whom he was involved in devil worship was none other than Madame de Montespan, the king's mistress.

There are two theories to explain the king's action in locking up Dauger. One is that he was protecting his mistress's reputation by removing Dauger to a safe place where he could not start malicious rumours about her bent for practising the black arts. The other is that the king was inflamed by a terrible fit of jealousy.

However, if either of these theories is true, why did Louis XIV not kill Dauger? There is still no satisfactory explanation for the extraordinary vengeance of the king in locking him up for so long and in forcing him to wear the terrible mask. While we may now know who he was, the mystery of the Man in the Iron Mask is as complete today as it was all those years ago when his guards removed from his cell all trace of his existence and buried him in an unmarked grave.

Spontaneous Human Combustion

Early on the frosty morning of 5 December 1966, Don Gosnell, a gas meter reader, started his day's work in the town of Coudersport, Pennsylvania. One of the first calls of the day was at was the home of Dr John Irving Bentley, a retired family doctor. Knowing that the 92-year-old physician could get about only with the aid of a walking frame, Gosnell was not surprised when no one answered the door, so he let himself in. In the hallway he detected a faint smell of smoke but took little notice.

Gosnell went straight down to the meters in the basement, where he noticed a neat pile of ash on the floor. He briefly wondered how it had got there but did not bother to turn his eyes upwards towards the ceiling, where there was a charred hole through which the ash had fallen from the bathroom above. Gosnell read the meter and walked back upstairs. Now there was a light blue smoke in the air.

Calling out for Dr Bentley, the meter man retraced his steps through the hallway towards the old man's bedroom. It was smoky but empty, so he headed for the bathroom. At the bathroom door he sniffed 'a strange, sweetish smell'. He then opened the door and immediately recoiled in horror at the sight that met his eyes.

Alongside the char-edged hole in the floor lay Dr Bentley's steel walking frame, blackened but with its rubber tips still intact. Beside the frame was the lower half of the doctor's right leg. A slipper was still on one of the old man's feet, which was burned off at the calf. And that was all that was left of Dr Bentley apart from a pile of ash. Don Gosnell ran from the building screaming: 'Dr Bentley is burned up!'

At the inquest which followed, the coroner listened to the seemingly obvious explanation that Dr Bentley had set himself on fire while lighting his pipe. This failed to tally with the facts, however, since the doctor's pipe was carefully placed on its stand by the bed. Neither did it explain why a fire of such ferocity had done so little damage to the rest of the bathroom which was virtually untouched by fire apart from a slight blackening on the side of the bathtub.

The coroner recorded a verdict of 'death by asphyxiation and 90 per cent burning of the body'. Hardly an explanation for one of the most macabre phenomena of our time. All the coroner would say after the case was: 'It was the oddest thing you ever saw.'

What the coroner did NOT mention was the phrase that has cropped up so often over the years in attempts to explain the fiery mystery of instant conflagration of a human body. Scientists today may dismiss it as fantasy, but our ancestors quite regularly spoke and wrote about this dreadful curse – this consumption by fire, this spontaneous human combustion.

One of the earliest, well-documented cases of spontaneous human combustion was the death of the 62-year-old Countess Cornelia Baudi, near Verona, in April 1731. We only know about the case because a friend of hers, a young priest, immediately put pen to paper to draft a dramatic account of the lady's demise.

The countess had enjoyed a quiet evening before retiring to bed. For an hour she chatted to her maid then fell into a deep sleep. In the morning the maid returned to her chamber but, even before entering, smelled a foul aroma. Inside the room the servant found the bedsheets turned back neatly as if the countess had just risen from her bed. The bedchamber and the bed itself were undamaged – yet the air was thick with soot, covering every surface. Horrified, the maid called for help and the priest came running. This was his account of the scene:

'The floor of the chamber was thick-smear'd with a gluish moisture, not easily got off . . . and from the lower part of the window trickl'd down a greasy, loathsome, yellowish liquor with an unusual stink. Four feet from the bed was a heap of ashes, two legs untouch'd, stockings on, between which lay the head, the brains, half of the back-part of the skull and the whole chin burn'd to ashes, among which were found three fingers blacken'd. All the rest was ashes which had this quality, that they left in the hand a greasy and stinking moisture . . .'

Another of the early, best documented cases of SHC also comes from Italy, but this time it was a priest who was the victim. The priest, named Bertholi, died in the town of Filetto, where a surgeon recounted the circumstances. Bertholi, who was on a visit to his brother-in-law, was alone in his room reading a prayer book when fearful screams were heard throughout the house. The priest was found on the floor engulfed by a pale, blue flame which receded as the surgeon and other witnesses entered the room. As the dying man writhed in agony, the surgeon was able to examine him and found that the man's flesh was burned to shreds – yet the sackcloth which he wore next to his skin was left entirely intact.

Many nations, including the Italians, have always studied SHC and taken the phenomenon seriously. But it was not until the nineteenth century that doctors in Britain and the United States even began to admit that such a fearsome mystery existed without a hint of scientific explanation. The study of SHC was aided by author Charles Dickens, who wrote of it in his novel Bleak House in 1833. The grisly death which his character Krook suffers in the book is believed to have been based upon the Italian case of Countess Baudi.

Two cases in the eighteenth century – one in Britain and one in the United States – well illustrate this gruesome enigma.

In 1841 the death of a 40-year-old woman was reported in the *British Medical Journal*. The woman had fallen near her hearth and was found still burning. By the time the fire was extinguished, the bones of her leg were carbonised – yet her stockings were entirely undamaged. And at Ayer, Massachusetts in 1880 an eminent physician was among several people in the company of woman when flames suddenly burst from her torso and legs. She sank to the ground and died in a fierce blaze.

The most renowned case of the early twentieth century occurred in 1919 when a well-known author, J. Temple Thurston, died at his country home in Kent. He was found in his armchair, the lower half of his body horribly burned – while the rest of his body was untouched. Indeed, Mr Temple Thurston had blazed away beneath his clothes without even singeing them.

Since then, coroners' courts have been seeking

more scientific explanations for phenomenon of spontaneous human combustion. In the nineteenth century, it was accepted that SHC, although a conundrum of science, was nevertheless a fact of life. As the twentieth century advanced, however, scientists became sceptical about the phenomenon and cases of it were rarely treated seriously. However, there was little in the way of scientific explanation offered in the following, baffling cases of the mid-war years.

In 1938 an American, Mrs Mary Carpenter, was holidaying with her family aboard a boat on the English Norfolk Broads when she suddenly burst into flames and was reduced to ashes.

That same year 22-year-old Phyllis Newcombe was leaving a dance hall at Chelmsford, Essex, when blue flames suddenly engulfed her body and she was reduced to a pile of ashes within minutes. 'In all my experience I have never come across anything as remarkable as this,' admitted a baffled coroner.

In a similar case, nineteen-year-old Maybelle Andrews was dancing with her boyfriend at a club in London's Soho when flames suddenly shot from her chest and back. 'The flames seemed to come from within her body,' said her tearful boyfriend. Other dancers failed to beat them out and within minutes she was dead.

The most famous case of spontaneous human

combustion, however, must be that of Mrs Mary Reeser, who died in her apartment in St Petersburg, Florida, in 1951.

Mrs Reeser, a plump widow of 67, was believed to have fallen asleep in her armchair one evening. When her landlady entered the apartment with two workmen the following day, they encountered a fierce heat but only a few flickering flames inside. All that was left of the armchair were a few springs – but even less remained of Mrs Reeser.

The heat had shrunk her skull to the size of a baseball. Part of her backbone remained recognisable after the blaze. Apart from that, there was only a left foot, intact but burned off at the ankle. On the foot, untouched by fire, was a satin carpet slipper. A newspaper lay near the body, entirely unscorched with its date clearly visible: 2 July 1951.

An inquest into Mrs. Reeser's death could find no scientific cause of the fire. Evidence was given that the blaze which had consumed her had been more intense than the 2500°F needed to dispose of the corpses in the city's crematorium. Yet the fire had not extended by more than inches from the old woman's body.

Renowned forensic anthropologist Dr Wilton Krogman, of the University of Pennsylvania School Of Medicine, who had studied several fire investigations involving burned corpses and who conducted a special investigation into the Reeser case, wrote:

'I cannot conceive of such complete cremation without more burning of the apartment itself. In fact the apartment and everything in it should have been consumed. Never have I seen a human skull shrunk by intense heat. The opposite has always been true; the skulls have been abnormally swollen or have virtually exploded into hundreds of pieces.

'I regard it as the most amazing thing I have ever seen. As I review it, the short hairs on my neck bristle with vague fear. Were I living in the Middle Ages, I would mutter something about black magic.'

What was once dismissed as just a mediaeval superstition had once again baffled the modern world of twentieth century science. Confronted with the mysterious phenomenon of spontaneous human combustion, the experts can still only admit defeat.

The Money Pit

A tiny island off the Canadian coast conceals one of the strangest mysteries on earth. For two centuries hopeful prospectors have sought buried treasure there in what is known as the Money Pit. Many have sunk their life savings in the venture; others have paid with their lives.

The Money Pit is located on Oak Island, in Mahone Bay, Nova Scotia. Its story began one day in 1795 when Daniel McGinnis, aged sixteen, gently paddled his canoe across the bay to one of the uninhabited islands. The one he alighted on was Oak Island.

He wandered from the beach to a small clearing where an old, gnarled oak stood, showing the signs of having been scarred by rope and tackle. On the ground in the clearing was a circular depression about 4.8 metres in diameter. Being a youngster brought up on the tales seafarers told about swashbuckling pirates, Daniel was immediately convinced that he had hit on a clearing where treasure had been buried, the oak bearing the scars of a makeshift crane that had been used to deposit the valuables deep inside the earth.

Daniel rowed back to the mainland to tell his

friends, Anthony Vaughan, aged thirteen, and John Smith, twenty. They went back to Oak Island next day armed with picks and shovels. They began to dig, realising that they were in a circular chamber of some kind that still bore pick marks on its smooth clay sides. At 1.2 metres they hit a floor of flagstones. They removed these on the first day and, over a period of a week, dug deeper and deeper, hitting a layer of close-packed logs at 3 metres, 6 metres and 9 metres intervals, each one of which they removed.

The three friends, disillusioned but nonetheless completely intrigued by what they had found, realised they could not continue with the tools at their disposal, and headed back for the mainland. They made a pledge to return.

It was to be nine years before John Smith returned with his friends, having persuaded a syndicate, backed by a well-off local man, Simeon Lynds, to finance a full-scale operation to search the pit. They were glad to see, on their return, that the shaft seemed to be as they had left it.

The excavation then began in earnest, with the help of a local labour force brought into the syndicate in return for a share of the treasure if and when it was discovered. More oak platforms were found as the shaft was sunk deeper: at 12 metres, at 15.2 metres, and at 18.2 metres (this one sealed with coconut fibre and putty). At 21.3

metres they hit plain oak, at 24.4 metres another platform of putty-sealed oak, and at 27.4 metres a stone of a kind not found in Nova Scotia, and bearing an inscription.

Smith, who by that time had bought Oak Island, fitted the stone in his fireplace. The significance, if any, of the illegible writing was lost on him and the other fortune hunters.

After wedging the stone out, the trio discovered yet another protective layer of wood. They were convinced that under this lay the treasure chest that would make them rich. It was by now nightfall; since water logging was becoming more and more of a problem the deeper they got, they decided to abandon the quest until daylight.

The following day was a Sunday and, being religious men, they did not work on the shaft, returning on Monday morning instead – only to find it flooded to ten metres from the top. They began bailing, and pressed an old pump into service. But no matter how much water they emptied out, the level in the shaft remained constant at ten metres depth from the top.

They abandoned the workings for a year, returning to their farms until the following spring, when they hit upon the idea of burrowing a separate new shaft alongside the original to take out the water. When they got down to 33.5

metres they tunnelled across into the original shaft – and were lucky to escape with their lives. The walls gave in and the new shaft also flooded, again to within ten metres of the top.

Smith and his partners, exasperated, gave up. They blamed their misfortune on nature and cursed their luck. The treasure remained out of their grasp.

It wasn't until 1849 that a second concerted bid was made to excavate the pit. A consortium of wealthy Nova Scotians calling itself the Truro Syndicate banded together to have another crack. Included in the Truro Syndicate was Anthony Vaughan, one of the original searchers, and Dr David Lynds, a relative of Simeon Lynds.

They re-dug the original shaft, getting it down to a depth of 26.2 metres. There was no problem with water. They called a halt on a Saturday night, attended church on Sunday, returned after the service – and found 18.2 metres of water in the shaft. They were back at square one.

After trying various pumping and bailing methods, the Truro Syndicate opted to employ a drill named a pod auger, which was driven by a horse and which could bring up materials and soil samples from below. Borings made by the drill, the latest of its kind and used in mining surveys of the day, produced clay, gravel, mud and sand.

To the east of the pit, at a depth of 32.3 metres,

they found fragments of oak, 56 centimetres of metal, more oak, more metal, more oak and finally spruce, before striking the clay bed. A jarring motion as the drill went down induced the searchers to believe that it had brushed by two treasure chests, one on top of the other.

There then occurred an event, no explanation for which has ever been found, but which could be a vital clue in the puzzle. The drilling foreman, a man named James Pitblado, was accused of taking something shiny from the drill as he scooped out the items brought up in the bit. The men, furious, demanded that he produce it, but he refused, pledging to reveal whatever it was to the directors of the syndicate the next time a full meeting was held.

Pitblado later tried to buy the entire eastern end of Oak Island, hopeful that he could then launch his own drilling operations. Legend has it that Pitblado dragged out a jewel, but he vanished soon afterwards, and whether he had a gemstone or not remains a mystery.

In 1850 a new shaft was sunk. After what looked like success, the water flooded back in again as the treasure-seekers tunnelled sideways into the original shaft of the Money Pit. It was only after this mishap that they set about solving the problem of the flooding. Samples taken from the drilling apparatus had shown them that the clay was impervious to water. One of the diggers tasted the moisture on his hand – and found it to be salt water.

The Money Pit was being flooded by the sea, and on a nearby beach the treasure-seekers discovered the amazing secret of the Money Pit. They saw that as the tide receded, the sand 'seemed almost to suck the water down, like the earth was thirsty,' as one digger put it.

Whoever had dug the Money Pit had also constructed a drainage system under the beach, intended to flood the shaft if ever it was breached to a certain depth. Digging down, they found the same coconut fibre, and then kelp grass over a tunnel of stones, which led back in the direction of the pit.

The idea behind the tunnel was both simple and brilliant. The coconut fibre and kelp grass allowed water to run into the sluice which led to the pit, but kept the clogging sand out. The stone tunnel led straight back to the pit at a depth of around 30 metres. As long as the shaft stayed full of earth, the pressure kept the water back. But as soon as the diggers reached it, the force of the water burst through, sealing the secret of the pit in a watery tomb. Poor Smith, all those years ago, had not been beaten by nature, but by an elaborate engineering system designed to keep people out of that great hole in the earth. Why?

At first the prospectors began construction of a dam, but that was smashed by an unusually high tide. Next they tried to block the tunnel, digging another shaft, the fifth to date, near to the site of the Money Pit. Water flooded in at 10.7 metres after they dislodged a boulder.

They thought they had intercepted the tunnel from the beach, but experience should have told them that they were not deep enough. Wood was driven in to stem the flow of water, a sixth shaft was sunk and, at 36 metres, as a tunnel was again being dug sideways into the original shaft, the whole thing collapsed.

It was to be a further nine years before the syndicate, which had already poured $20,000 down the pit to no avail, tried again. More shafts were sunk, the pit still flooded, a man was scalded to death when a steam pump blew up – and still there was no sign of any treasure.

Soon the area around the Money Pit looked like a building site, as amateurs and experts alike sunk shaft after shaft in the quest for riches. It was all to no avail.

Over the years, several companies were formed to plumb the depths of the Money Pit. One used dynamite to dam the tunnels connecting the pit with the sea in a vain bid to prevent the flooding. Another team struck metal, and a fragment brought to the surface on the bit contained a piece of parchment on which the letters 'V.I.' could be clearly made out. Another explorer published 'proof' that maps drafted by the infamous pirate Captain Kidd pointed to his treasure having been buried there.

In 1963 the pit claimed its worst casualties. On 17 August Robert Restall was overcome by the exhaust fumes of his pump, and both he, his son, John, and two other men who tried to rescue him died. In 1965 Robert Dunfield squandered $120,000 succeeding in making more huge holes. There have been several attempts since then, including one adventurer who swam up the deep flood tunnel to try to find the treasure.

Who built this amazing feat of engineering? One author who has studied the Money Pit thinks that it was the work of British Army engineers during the American War of Independence. Rupert Furneaux, who has written an authoritative account of the pit called *Money Pit: The Mystery of Oak Island*, claims that they buried money there in case of a reversal in the war's fortunes. But this does not answer the question of what happened to the money. Nor are there British Army records of such an enterprise.

The secret lies in the mud, along with the bodies, sweat and money which have been spent vainly trying to find the secret of the Money Pit.

Caspar Hauser

There was something about the boy that made him stand out from the throng. Aged about sixteen, he was shabbily dressed. He wore a cut-down frock coat with tattered breeches and split boots held together with horseshoe nails. He shuffled nervously, with faltering steps, across one of the grander squares of the German city of Nuremberg on a Whit Monday holiday of 26 May 1828.

Perhaps it was the boots that made George Weichmann, a cobbler, pay particular attention to the boy. Or perhaps it was a paternal streak in the gentle cobbler. Whatever the reason, he approached the youth – and heard him whimpering softly to himself, apparently oblivious to his surroundings.

The boy's response to Weichmann's questions of concern were unintelligible; it was as if he did not understand a word. Instead he thrust at him an envelope bearing the legend: 'The Captain of the 4th Squadron, 6th Cavalry Regiment.'

Weichmann took the sealed envelope and led the strange youth to the captain's residence nearby. The captain was not at home but his servant invited the shoemaker and his new companion to wait for his master's return.

Meanwhile the servant offered them food. The strange youngster turned up his nose at fine beer, food and the famous little sausages of the town when they were produced for him – but wolfed down plain brown bread and water.

He managed to grunt a few words to the shoemaker when he asked who he was and where he came from. He replied: 'I want to be a soldier, like father . . . horse . . . home . . . father.' And he pointed to his feet, encased in the shabby boots, and cried, as in pain.

The captain arrived presently, provoking great interest in the young man, who was obviously excited by his uniform. Weichmann handed the captain the envelope, which turned out to contain not one but two letters.

The first purported to be written by a labourer into whose charge the unfortunate boy had been delivered in 1812. He said that he could no longer look after him, as he had ten other children and could not support Caspar as well. He also said that the boy, since being deposited with him (it did not make clear why or how) had spent the whole time locked up in his house, with no contact with the outside world.

The letter was dated 1828 and ended: 'If his parents had lived he might have been well educated; for if you show him anything he can do it right off.'

The second letter was dated sixteen years earlier, in 1812, and purported to be from the boy's natural mother. 'Take care of my child,' read the scrawl. 'He has been baptised. His father was a soldier in the 6th Cavalry.'

This was too much for the captain, who turned the boy over to the city authorities, who in turn gave him over to the police as a waif. They locked him in a cell, where a jailer made the curious observation:

'He can and does sit for hours without moving a limb. He does not pace the floor nor does he try to sleep. He sits rigidly without growing in the least uncomfortable. Also, he prefers darkness to light and can move about in it like a cat.'

He was given a piece of paper upon which he scratched just three words. One was *Reiter*, German for cavalryman. The other two words were 'Caspar Hauser'.

Among his meagre possessions were found a black silk neckerchief and a white handkerchief with the initials 'C.H.' worked in red in one of the corners. He was immediately named Caspar Hauser, although there was not one single tangible clue as to his identity or to where he originated from.

One kind jailer took Caspar into his own private apartment and observed the boy unseen. He thought him a creature of childlike actions, but believed there lay behind his apparent imbecility a stronger, more intelligent force. Caspar could sulk like a baby, but when amused or interested his face positively beamed with an engaging smile. He walked like a child, too, overbalancing and unsteady as though he had had little practice of this most elementary of human skills. It was as if he had had very little contact with people or with the outside world.

His attentive jailer provided Caspar with a toy wooden horse which the boy loved, and within six weeks he had learned a string of new words, showing an impressive eagerness to learn and an innate, natural intelligence. He set about introducing his protégé to the outside world.

In the nineteenth century the gracious German city of Nuremberg was the epitome of a provincial centre slowly coming to terms with the great changes brought about by the industrial revolution. The second city of Bavaria, after Munich, it enjoyed the distinction of being replete with fine buildings and many art treasures. It was known as the treasure house of Germany.

But it was not Nuremberg's churches, or its paintings or sculptures, which rocketed it to European fame in 1828. It was the arrival of the jailer's protégé. Such a curiosity – as he emerged into a world intrigued by fables and the extra-ordinary — made Caspar the talk of Nuremberg.

Within six weeks, the shabbily clad waif from nowhere was the talk of all Germany.

Caspar's fame impelled the Burgomeister of Nuremberg to don his official robes to visit him. His purpose was to elicit the secrets of Caspar's past; and, while he was not much enlightened, he was certainly not at all disappointed by the tale Caspar Hauser had to tell.

Caspar said he had lived all his life in a tiny cell 1.8 metres long, 1.4 metres wide and 1.7 metres high. The windows were permanently shuttered, he slept on a straw mattress, his feet were kept bare. His only nourishment was bread and water, and he said that the water often tasted bitter. When it did, he recalled falling asleep immediately after drinking it. After sleeping, he would find a clean shirt in his cell, placed next to the two wooden horses and wooden dogs that were left for him to play with.

A mysterious man was behind all this. Caspar said he never saw his face, but before he was turned out and sent to Nuremberg, the man, wearing a mask, showed Caspar how to trace the letters of the words Caspar Hauser.

Finally, Caspar recalled how he was taught to stand and walk. He said he had been given the letters and then set about his journey to Nuremberg, an odyssey about which he could remember nothing except the pain in his feet.

The Nuremberg council published this account in a much edited text, and the document on the 'Child of Nuremberg' took Caspar's story to the far corners of Europe and beyond. He became, in twentieth century parlance, a celebrity.

An appeal was sent out from the city fathers for information about Caspar. Rumours flourished – not least that he had been shut away because he was the illegitimate son of royalty.

Occultists said he came from the Devil, while fortune tellers and mystics blamed Caspar's arrival on beings from another world. And there were those, too, who denounced him as a charlatan and a con-man. Whatever the reality, the authorities entrusted to trace his whereabouts were stumped.

While these searches continued, Caspar was placed into the care of George Daumer, a professor noted for his work in education and philosophy. Daumer was impressed by Caspar. Caspar had a finely attuned, almost animal sense of smell. He could see well in the dark, identify trees by sniffing the air, and soon learned to write and draw extremely well.

What seemed to baffle him were elementary physical phenomena of the age. He would even try to pinch the flames of burning candles, recoiling in pain when the fire burned him.

Like John Merrick, the Elephant Man, who

drew crowds of visitors eager to gawp at something so utterly different from the norm, Caspar Hauser became a sideshow figure, receiving at his apartment in Professor Daumer's home the elite of German drawing room society.

Caspar seemed to revel in the attention showered upon him. The visits of educated men and women fuelled their interests and suspicions, which soon fell on the Duke of Baden who was believed to have cruelly imprisoned Caspar because he was his bastard son. Needless to say, such charges have never been proved.

In October 1829, some three months after Professor Daumer had set himself the task of writing a full and detailed biography of Caspar, there was a startling development.

On the seventh of that month Caspar was discovered unconscious, with a stab wound in his head, in the cellar of the professor's home. He said, when he came round, that he had been attacked by a man wearing a black mask. The news was electric, fuelling rumours once again that someone, somewhere, probably highly placed, had loosed an assassin on the unfortunate Caspar to silence him in case he revealed details of his past. The cynics, naturally, said the wound was self-inflicted.

Nevertheless, Caspar was moved from the custody of the benevolent Professor Daumer and given into the care of the city. He was placed at a secret address, under police guard, and for two years enjoyed the benefits of being looked after out of the public purse – a situation of which even the citizens of Nuremberg soon tired.

The story could have ended here, with Caspar being put back upon the highways, had it not been for the arrival in May 1831 of the eccentric Englishman Lord Stanhope, who came to Nuremberg and virtually adopted Caspar. He persuaded the city authorities to allow him to become his guardian, and he promised to look into the boy's past.

Sadly, Stanhope treated Caspar more like a sideshow freak than an enigma to be deciphered; he touted him around the minor courts of Europe, and the relationship between the two was less than harmonious.

In 1833 he took him to Ansbach, 25 kilometres from Nuremberg, to lodge in the care of Pastor Meyer, a suspicious, mean-minded man who employed a bodyguard named Hickel to watch over Caspar. Hickel was a thug but restrained from harming Caspar because of the enormous public and royal interest in him.

Both Stanhope and Meyer, however, seemed to lose interest in the boy. Stanhope left him in the permanent care of Meyer in 1833. And Meyer himself virtually abandoned him some months later after he failed to acquit himself well in the Latin and religious studies he had been set.

On 11 December 1833 Caspar Hauser was savagely attacked by an unknown assailant as he walked in a local park. He staggered back to Meyer's house, bleeding profusely. In his great pain he managed to communicate that he had been stabbed by a man who had asked him his name. Upon hearing it he had plunged a knife into his ribs.

Meyer refused to believe Caspar – but three days later Caspar Hauser died, denying that he had killed himself and maintaining that he was not an impostor.

Before Caspar's assassin had run off, he had dropped a black wallet which the police later found. In it was a note, written in mirror writing, which said:

'Hauser will be able to tell you how I look, whence I came from and who I am. To spare him the task, I will tell you myself. I am from . . . on the Bavarian border . . . on the river . . . My name is MLO.'

And that, in effect, was the last scrap of evidence about Caspar Hauser. He was buried in a quiet country churchyard. His gravestone read: 'Here lies Caspar Hauser, enigma. His birth was unknown, his death mysterious.'

Ever since the arrival in Nuremberg of Caspar

Hauser (if, indeed, that was his true name) there has been unending exploration into his past. Was he an impostor, a royal prince, an alien being, a true waif? Researchers have come to the same dead end. Caspar Hauser is as mysterious today as he was when he hobbled into the square in Nuremberg in those painful boots.

The Yeti

In 1832 the British explorer B. H. Hodgson travelled deep into the Himalayas to record the lifestyle of the Nepalese. In one letter home he told how the tribespeople lived in fear of a mysterious, tall, erect creature covered in thick black hair. In one incident reported to Hodgson, porters had fled in terror from this animal. They called it the 'Rakshas' – Sanskrit for demon.

Hodgson himself was scathing of the eye-witness accounts. He believed the porters had probably seen a stray orang-utan. But as the years passed by, evidence of an unknown creature living in one of the world's last great wildernesses was mounting.

Though he hadn't realised it, Hodgson had been first to tell the Western World of the possible existence of the Yeti.

It was 50 years before the mystery was revived in the West, courtesy of Major L Waddell of the Indian Army Medical Corps. He told of seeing large footprints which, it was claimed, belonged to 'one of the hairy men who live in the eternal snows'. Waddell however was also sceptical, believing the Yeti were in fact snow bears.

In his book *Among the Himalayas* he reported: 'The belief in these creatures is

Nepal. Tracks in the snow thought to be from a dark
ape-like creature spotted by British climber Don
Whillans while climbing Mount Annapurna.

universal among Tibetans. None, however, of the Tibetans I have interrogated on the subject could ever give me an authentic case. On the most superficial investigation it always resolved into something that somebody had heard tell of.'

Then in 1914 a British forestry official, J. R. P. Gent, told of discovering bizarre footprints near a remote lodge in Sikkim. He noted: 'The peculiar feature is that its tracks are about 18 to 24 inches long and the toes point in the opposite direction to that in which the animal is moving. I take it that he walks on his knees and shins instead of on the souls of his feet.'

Gent's observations were largely ignored at home. There was, after all, a war on and men with a taste for adventure were rushing to sign up for king and country. But during the 1920s his account was given a much wider circulation. One newspaper referred to the unknown creature as the 'Abominable Snowman'. This phrase gripped the public's imagination and soon there were dozens of mountaineering expeditions heading for the Himalayas. Many climbers claimed to have seen the Snowman. None produced any hard evidence.

But some of the sightings simply could not be put down to over-active imaginations. The photographer N. A. Tombazi saw a Yeti in the spring of 1925 when he was climbing the Zemu

Is this what a Yeti really looks like? In fact, it is a model constructed from eye-witness reports.

glacier. It was about 300 yards away in a low valley and at first the sunlight glaring off the snow made it almost impossible for him to describe. Slowly, as his eyes adjusted to the intense light, the image became clearer. His account later appeared in the book *Bigfoot* by author John Napier.

As a Fellow of the British Royal Geographical Society, Tombazi is deservedly regarded as one of the most reliable witnesses in the whole Yeti mystery. A seasoned traveller, he was certainly well aware of the tricks which light could sometimes play. He also knew the importance of accurate observation.

Tombazi told how one of the Sherpas spotted the creature and drew his attention to it. This is how he described the next few moments:

'Unquestionably the figure in outline was exactly like a human being, walking upright and stopping occasionally to uproot or pull at some dwarf rhododendron bushes. It showed up dark against the snow and, as far as I could make out, wore no clothes. Within the next minute or so it had moved into some thick scrub and was lost to view. Such a fleeting glimpse, unfortunately, did not allow me to set the telephoto camera, or even to fix the object carefully with my binoculars.

'But a couple of hours later, during the descent, I purposely made a detour so as to pass

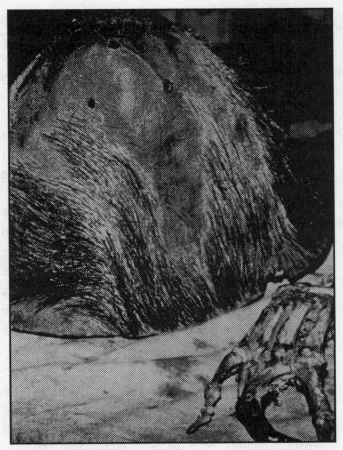

Scalp and hand, purported to be from a Yeti, kept at Pangboche Monastery, Nepal.

the place where the man or beast had been seen. I examined the footprints which were clearly visible on the surface of the snow. They were similar in shape to those of a man. The prints were undoubtedly bi-ped, having no characteristics whatever of any imagined quadruped. From inquiries I made a few days later at Yokson on my return journey, I gather that no man had gone in that direction since the beginning of the year.'

Tombazi's account was given added weight by the 1936 expedition of Ronald Kaulback, who also reported seeing giant footprints. The following year the first photograph of the mysterious tracks were published, though this actually proved very little. The Abominable Snowman remained as he had always been – both reclusive and elusive.

On 8 November 1951 another highly-regarded witness emerged in the form of the respected mountaineer and naturalist Eric Shipton. He and his British colleague Michael Ward, together with their Sherpa, Sen Tensing, came across some perfect tracks 18,000 feet up the Men-lung glacier in the Gauri Sankar mountain range.

Shipton judged that the 13 by 8 inch print was made by a flat-footed beast up to 8 feet tall. He produced photographs of a second trail, later dismissed by critics as goat hoof-prints which had expanded in the heat of the sun. This theory was itself ridiculed by many eminent scientists. Besides, Shipton was an acknowledged world expert on animal tracks and not a man to reach conclusions lightly.

Throughout the 1950s the hunt went on. Everest conqueror Sir Edmund Hillary was deeply sceptical of the Yeti's existence, yet sufficiently intrigued to mount his own expedition in 1960. He returned with a scalp claimed to have been hacked from a Yeti. Zoologists identified it as goat antelope hair yet it was still a valuable specimen. The hair contained a type of parasite unknown to scientists.

Right up to the present day reports have continued to filter in. Careful analysis shows certain common threads which will undoubtedly prove invaluable for future expeditions.

The Yeti appears to live at heights of between 12,000 feet and 20,000 feet, preferring dense forests close to the seasonal snow line. Nepalese villagers believe they live mainly in caves, venturing out mainly in darkness but occasionally driven by hunger to hunt for food in the daytime. Some witnesses claim the creature is twelve feet high and extremely agile; others put it considerably smaller and talk of it lolloping along swinging its arms.

The head is apparently conical with facial characteristics somewhere between humans and apes. The fur is thick and red and covers every part of the body except the face. The creature's diet is rumoured to be mainly rodents and lichen and they apparently show the curiously human trait of disembowelling meat before beginning their meal.

It is all fascinating stuff. But what about the oh-so-elusive hard evidence? To the surprise of sceptics, this too has now been presented – though not from the Yeti's traditional stamping ground. The hair samples which set anthropologists into fits of excitement came from across the Himalayas in China.

For decades China had sealed its borders to the West and it was not until the late 1980s that a more open view began to prevail in Beijing. This new mood set off a rush of scientific expeditions from the West, including one financed jointly by six countries, including the United Stases and Britain. The aim was to find evidence of the Wildman of China, a creature apparently similar to the Yeti and its North American equivalent, Bigfoot.

The party led by Gene Poirier, professor of Anthropology at Ohio State University, collected a number of hair samples. These had been found by farmers working some of the most remote regions of central China. Shanghai's Fudan University had already declared that the samples were not from any known man or ape.

At Ohio and at Birmingham University in England, researchers used special electron microscopes to establish that the hairs contained 54 times as much zinc and iron as human hairs, and 8 times as much as animal hairs. Professor Poirier, an avowed sceptic of Yeti-type creatures declared: 'We have established that the animal does not fall into any known category. This is the first evidence of the existence of a new, higher primate.'

Critical observers still question why, in an age of ever-expanding technology, scientists have not been able to come up with some more concrete proof – a body or bones for example. The answer has been succinctly summed up by Richard Greenwell of the US based International Society of Cryptozoology. He observed: 'You would need 10,000 people to actually catch a Wildman because the area is so vast and densely forested. You could pass a yard from one and not know it was there.'

For the time being, at least, the mystery remains unsolved.

Black Holes

Black holes are one of the great mysteries of space. They are the powerhouses of the universe: forces of unimaginably concentrated energy. Their gravitational pull is so strong that even light cannot escape from them. If manned spacecraft were sent to distant planets, black holes would be among the greatest hazards faced on the journey.

Black holes, the collective name given to stars which have collapsed in on themselves, are as mysterious as they are fascinating. What little is known of the phenomena is largely due to theories painstakingly worked out by scientists and astronomers through recent years. As one eminent observer of the universe put it: 'Black holes are as pervasive in theory as they are evasive in observation.'

It was in the last century that experts began to piece together the puzzle of black holes. In life, a star contains almost inconceivable amounts of energy, so dense in matter that if it literally collapsed in on itself, the gravitational pull would be so strong that nothing, not even light, would escape from it. It would become invisible, the extraordinary gravitational pull allowing nothing whatever to escape from its clutches. Even light which passed near the black hole – from stars, planets, passing meteorites – would be sucked in and vanish forever.

The laws of nature as we know them on planet Earth would no longer apply in such an alien environment. The largest battleship ever built could be plunged into a black hole and it would stretch like a piece of elastic -- before disintegrating into a billion particles of matter. The matter itself would also disintegrate in time, leaving only the image of the battleship for all eternity on the outer fringes of the hole where the last dying particles of light linger.

If this scientific theory is hard to follow, consider the gravity of the Earth:

Were a man to fall from a skyscraper, he would plummet to his death, drawn irresistibly downwards by the Earth's gravitational pull. But it takes the whole gravitational pull of the entire planet to make even a feather fall downwards; so, relatively, gravity is a weak force.

However, if the Earth were condensed in size to something with the circumference of a tennis ball, it would be so dense that no light would be able to escape from it. The density would, say experts, be upwards of 3000 times that of known matter. And a ton of it would fit into a matchbox!

The stars nearest in structure to black holes are white dwarfs. They were discovered in the last century by the German-born astronomer Friedrich Bessel, who was studying the star Sirius, brightest in the galaxy. In 1844, using the most sophisticated telescope available to him, he noticed that Sirius' movement was wavy rather than in a straight line — as if some unseen force had a gravitational pull on it.

It was only twenty years later that an American astronomer spotted small diffusions of bright light while testing a new telescope. The white light indicated an intensely hot star which, by the rule applied then, suggested a huge mass. Yet the nature of the diffused light implied that, although it contained massive amounts of energy, it was small; only its mass was gigantic. This was the energy source christened 'white dwarf'.

Scientists believe that a star turns into a white dwarf in four stages. First, hydrogen in the star's core is fused into helium; and, after several billion years, all the hydrogen is used up. Second, the star's core contracts, its exterior expands and the star becomes a red giant. Third, the outer layers of the red giant are gradually expelled until, finally, all that remains is the super-dense mass of the white dwarf.

The black hole is one stage advanced from the white dwarf, where no light can be seen and the gravitational force is millions of times greater than anything we know. According to Einstein's famous theory of relativity, a black hole would appear infinite inside, and there would be no escape for anything.

Because there are so many stars in the universe capable of collapsing in on themselves and turning into black holes (scientists reckon up to 90 per cent), space travel could be exceptionally hazardous for manned craft.

Because of their very nature, no one has ever seen a black hole, although a great deal of research is going on to find them. At present scientists can only point to where some may be by applying Bessel's logic and studying those stars which seem to be affected by the gravitational force of an invisible body.

A further problem in studying black holes is that even if astronomers knew when a star was going to collapse in on itself, the event would occur so quickly that they would not have time to witness it. Professor John Taylor, a British mathematician, says in his book *Black Holes: The End of the Universe?* that a star ten times the size of our sun would fade from view in four millionths of a second, while one that was a million times heavier than the sun would vanish in one quarter of a second.

As black holes are sources of such immense energy, some scientists are investigating ways of harnessing that energy – a task which sounds, on the face of it, quite impossible. Cambridge genius Stephen Hawking argued that the extraordinary gravitational pull near the entrance to a black hole would be strong enough to split atoms into particles and anti-particles, which on Earth would mean that atoms would destroy themselves in much the same way as in a gigantic nuclear blast.

But because the laws of nature and science do not apply to black holes, one of the pair – particle and antiparticle – would escape back into the hole, and the process would be continued. If there were a way of harnessing this energy, argued Hawking, the effects could be extraordinary.

Other theorists argue that soon it might be possible to create a black hole in a laboratory, bringing to life the theories of Einstein, and giving mathematicians and astronomers perspectives on space never before realised. Professor Taylor, however, is one sceptic of such an experiment. According to his prediction, if a black hole weighing just sixteen tons were somehow artificially constructed in a laboratory, it would immediately sink to the centre of the Earth and destroy it, much as a black hole would destroy the unwary space traveller who strayed into it. Perhaps that is one experiment best left untried.

Albert Einstein went one stage further down the doomsday road. Since the universe is littered with black holes, he and many scientists have argued that eventually ALL galaxies risk collapsing in on themselves, turning the universe into one giant black hole. This would occur, according to Einstein, because of the 'big bang' theory – which surmises that the universe was formed by a gigantic explosion and is constantly expanding. If that is so, what is to stop it from flying apart?

Einstein said there must be enough mass in the universe to hold it together. This mass could be in the form of black holes, acting as the counter-weights to the big bang and drawing the stars and planets back towards them. Taken to its logical conclusion, the black holes would eventually consume everything – and our universe would simply disappear!

Bigfoot

The first frontiersmen who braved the wilderness in the north-west of America were also the first white men to hear the amazing stories of wild, hairy beasts of the woods. Throughout the forests and mountains that covered the uncharted terrain, from California in the south to Alaska in the north, lurked an awesome creature that struck fear into even the bravest settler. According to the Indians whose domain this once was, these man-like beasts of no known species were about eight feet tall, with broad chest and shoulders but virtually no neck. They were covered in auburn hair and walked with a stoop. It was known by the Indians as Sasquatch – later named by the white man as Bigfoot.

The reason for the beast's new name became clear to the world in the nineteenth century when explorer David Thomas discovered evidence of the strange animal, in the shape of footprints, at least fourteen inches long, near Jasper, Alberta.

In 1851 the first recorded newspaper report of such creature was published in Arkansas, far from where most Bigfoot sightings have since been made. The creature, which was seen chasing a herd of cattle, was described as 'an animal

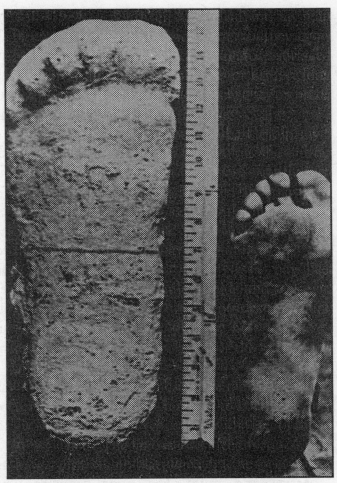

Plaster cast belonging to a creature of unknown origin compared to the foot of an adult human male.

bearing the unmistakable likeness of humanity, thought to be a survivor of the earthquake which devastated the area in 1811'. The report went on: 'He was of a gigantic stature, the body being covered with hair and the head with long locks that fairly enveloped the neck and shoulders. The wild man, after looking at them deliberately for a short time, turned and ran away with great speed, leaping twelve to fourteen feet at a time. His footprints measured thirteen inches each.'

In 1884 *The Colonist*, the principal newspaper for British Columbia, gave an account of the capture of a Sasquatch. This creature, nicknamed Jacko by the local settlers, was spotted by the crew of a train travelling along the Fraser River from the town of Lytton to Yale. They pursued it, captured it by knocking it unconscious with a rock and, having locked it in the guard's van, took it into Yale.

There it was examined and was described as being 'gorilla-like, with coarse black hair' except for its hands and feet. It was presumed to be a young Sasquatch, as it was only 4 feet and 7 inches tall and weighed 127 pounds. It's diet was berries and milk. The poor creature was exhibited in the Yale area before being sold to Barnum and Bailey's Circus. But Sasquatch Junior is said to have died in his crate while on the long rail journey to his new circus home.

The Bigfoot stories gained ultimate credibility, however, in 1903 when no less a person than President Theodore Roosevelt retold the story of two trappers in the Salmon River district of Idaho who were attacked by a mysterious creature.

Then, in 1918 the *Seattle Times* reported a dramatic attack by 'mountain devils' on a prospector on Mount St Helen, Washington. In the same state, a lumber camp worker came face-to-face with a large 'ape-like' beast. It was 50 years later that Albert M. Fletcher sat down to record the encounter. He wrote:

'In the fall of 1917 when I was seventeen years old I was working for a lumber camp on the Cowlitz River. One moonlit evening, I was walking down a logging road en route to a dance when I had the uneasy feeling that something was following close behind me. I kept looking over my shoulder but could not see anything. When I came to a bend in the road I ducked behind a tree and waited to see what it was. Almost immediately a very large man-like creature about six-and-a-half or seven feet tall came into view.

'It was walking on its hind legs, was covered with dark hair, had a bearded face and a large chest and, so far as I could see, was not wearing clothes of any kind. Startled, I let out a yell of alarm and the creature instantly turned and ran off into the woods, still on its hind legs. I told some of my co-workers about it and some of them laughed but others said they too had seen it. No one had an explanation for it and no name was given to it, but all agreed that it was a large, ape-like something and that it also resembled a very large man.'

Of all encounters with Bigfoot, the most dramatic was reported in 1924 by Albert Ostman, also a lumberman, from Langley, British Columbia. Ostman was camping opposite Vancouver Island when he was abducted by a giant Bigfoot. Ostman said the beast (about eight feet tall) picked him up, still in his sleeping bag, and carried him 'like a sack of potatoes' for three hours. As dawn broke, he realised that they had reached the creature's lair.

Ostman now surveyed his captors. He was being held by four Bigfoot: male and female adults and a pair of male and female children. Dumped in their lair, the lumberman still had his rifle with him but was reluctant to use it since the ape-like family had done him no harm. He also still had a few cans of food and other provisions that were buried in his sleeping bag. Some of these he ate while the Bigfoot family dined on spruce tips, sweet grass and roots. The woodsman was allowed the freedom of the valley in which he was held, although always followed by at least two of the creatures.

Eventually, fearing that he had been kidnapped as a possible husband for one of the children, he determined to escape. He fed the largest Bigfoot some snuff and, while the creature rushed to bury his face in a stream, Ostman fled. He had been held captive for an entire week but, fearing ridicule, did not immediately tell his story. And when he did, it seemed incredible – except for the many later pieces of evidence which backed his descriptions of the beastly Bigfoot.

Another encounter the same year was reported from the area now known as Ape Canyon, on the Oregon-Washington border. When prospectors there shot and killed one of a group of Bigfoot, the survivors attacked their camp, causing considerable damage but no serious injury. Reporters who later visited the site told of seeing hundreds of giant footprints. The man who had fired the first shot, Fred Beck, gave a full version of the attack to Dr John Napier, author of the fascinating book *Bigfoot*. Napier tells his story:

'At night the apes counter-attacked, opening the assault by knocking a heavy strip of wood out from between two logs of the miners' cabin. After that there were assorted poundings on the walls, door and roof but the building was designed to withstand heavy mountain snows and the apes failed to break in. The miners fired shots through the walls and roof without driving them away.

The noise went on from shortly after dark until nearly dawn. Mr Beck (could not) say that there were more than two creatures outside. There were that many because there had been one on the roof and one pounding the wall simultaneously. However many there were, it was enough for the miners, who packed up and abandoned their mine the next day.'

In 1933 two men observed a Bigfoot leisurely munching berries in a clearing at Pitt Lake, northern British Columbia. They described it as having 'a human-like face on a fur- clad body'. In the same province, the Chapman family, of Ruby Creek, fled their lonely farmhouse when a Bigfoot attacked it. But it lost interest and meandered away after overturning a barrel of salted fish.

In 1955 occurred one of the clearest-ever sightings of a Bigfoot. It was made at Mica Mountain, British Columbia, by William Roe from his vantage point behind a thick bush. Suddenly, out of the undergrowth appeared a female Bigfoot, about six feet tall and weighing around 300 pounds.

The giant creature approached Roe, unaware that she was being watched. When she got to within twenty feet of him she squatted down in front of the bush in which Roe was hiding, enabling him to make a thorough study of the beast. He was later able to describe in detail her enormous body, the shape of her head, what kind of face and hair she had and the way she walked. His report of the continued:

'Finally, the wild thing must have got my scent, for it looked directly at me through a small opening in the bush. Still in a crouched position, it backed up three or four short steps then straightened up to its full height and started to walk rapidly back the way it had come. For a moment it watched me over its shoulders as it went, not exactly afraid, but as though it wanted no contact with anything strange.'

Roe admitted that he had thought of shooting the creature as proof of its existence. He even got as far as raising his rifle and aiming – but he could not fire.

Further south, in Humboldt county, northern California, truck driver Jerry Crew found clear tracks of a Bigfoot in the mud. He took a plaster cast of one, and the photograph prompted fresh interest in the mystery.

At nearby Bluff Creek in 1958 a road construction worker encountered a Bigfoot which, he said, he could only get rid of by offering a candy bar. Later, construction site workers awoke one morning to find sixteen-inch footprints in the snow around their cabins at Bluff Creek. The distance between the prints meant that a creature or creatures had been prowling around during the night, taking strides of up to five feet. They also discovered that a 50-gallon fuel drum had been moved from one end of the camp to the other. A search party set out to hunt the beasts and picked one of them up in their truck headlights before losing it in dense woodland. In 1963 one of the creatures returned to Bluff Creek and attacked another construction site. A newspaper report at the time credited the beast with sufficient strength to overturn a truck.

The famed explorer and aptly named oilman, Tom Slick, whose passion had been hunting the Abominable Snowman of Nepal, now launched himself into the search for Bigfoot. But in 1963 he crashed in his private plane, the findings of his expeditions unrevealed.

The big breakthrough in the hunt for Bigfoot came on 20 October 1967. Roger Patterson, a former rodeo cowboy and rancher, was tracking the forests around Bluff Creek with an Indian friend, Bob Gimlin, when they emerged from woodland into a clearing – and came face to face with a Bigfoot. Patterson took his 16 mm movie camera from its case and aimed it at the beast as it ambled along the bank of the creek. He shot an amazing 29 feet of colour film as it loped across his field of vision. Patterson and Gimlin also took casts of footprints left by the creature.

The film was shown world-wide and most experts believed it to be genuine, although some disputed Patterson's belief that the creature was female. One copy was given to Bigfoot investigator Dr Napier, who was more sceptical. He wrote:

'The upper part of the body bears some resemblance to an ape and the lower half is typically human. It is almost impossible to conceive that such structural hybrids could exist in nature. One half of must be artificial.'

Other pieces of evidence were shown to Dr Napier over the years, principally the so-called 'Minnesota Iceman', a hairy gorilla-like humanoid at first said to have been found preserved in a 6000 pound block of ice in the Bering Straits. Later versions of its discovery had it being shot by hunters along the snowline of a north-western mountain. Dr Napier judged this specimen – as many others – to be 'transparently dubious'. This leading expert on Bigfoot does have the final, convincing word on the mystery, however. He wrote:

'The North American Bigfoot or Sasquatch has a lot going for it. Too many claim to have seen it, or at least to have seen footprints, to dismiss its reality out of hand. To suggest that hundreds of people at worst are lying or at best deluding themselves is neither proper nor realistic.'

The Secret of Rennes Le Chateau

The hamlet of Rennes Le Chateau sprawls across a hilltop on the outskirts of the Pyrénées, in southern France. It is a tightly-knit community of farm workers and grape pickers living in neat white cottages. The thin mountain air is filled with the swish of scythes and the call of birds. Life has not changed here for generations.

It was no different in the summer of 1891 when parish priest Berenger Sauniere began to renovate St Mary Magdalen Church on the hillside. He removed an altar stone resting across two columns and found that one of them was hollow. Inside were four tubes containing parchments. Nobody knows for sure what was written on all the documents, for some were in code. But they set the priest on a fabulous trail, an odyssey of mystery and adventure, a journey to a secret source of wealth.

Sauniere's pay was £6 a year. Yet he spent an astonishing £10 million on his church, on the village, on missionary work — and on himself. He refused to say where the money came from and the only person to share the secret, his housekeeper Marie, kept her silence to the grave.

Yet Father Berenger built a modern road up to the village. He piped in running water. He hired craftsmen from all over Europe to redecorate the church in a lurid fashion, with hideous statues and gaudy plaques. He constructed a lavish villa for himself and his housekeeper, with a tower and an orangery. He filled it with a collection of rare china, precious fabrics, antique marble and a magnificent library. He threw regular banquets for his parishioners and he gave cash handouts to the locals. He financed missionary work in Africa and he funded convents and monasteries.

He also entertained a constant flow of important guests, from Roman Catholic Church officials to politicians. One of his most frequent visitors was the Archduke Johann Von Hapsburg, a cousin of the emperor of Austria. It was subsequently found that Hapsburg and Sauniere had opened consecutively numbered bank accounts and that considerable sums of money had been transferred to the priest. In addition, this simple country priest had no fewer than seven bulging accounts in other banks across Europe.

Sauniere always refused to accept either promotion or a transfer, and an attempt to have him thrown out of the Church for illegally selling Masses was overruled by the Pope. In 1917, as Sauniere lay dying, a priest was called to hear his final confession. But the priest was so shocked by what Sauniere told him that he refused to give him absolution.

Not even Sauniere's will threw any light on the mystery, for it showed him to be penniless. He had given his wealth to his housekeeper Marie, who remained living in comfort at the villa until 1946, when the French government issued a new currency. Before the banks would exchange new francs for old, everyone was obliged to declare how they had obtained their money. Marie did not – and was seen in her garden burning bundles of the useless old notes. She chose to live in poverty rather than reveal her secret.

Eventually Marie sold the villa so that she could live on the proceeds of the deal. She promised the new owner, Noel Corbu, that she would tell her secret before she died. But in 1953 she suffered a stroke which left her incapable of speech and she died unable or unwilling to communicate the answer to the puzzle.

So how was it that Berenger Sauniere, who earned only £6 a year as a parish priest, was able to spend the £10 million in 25 years?

The most extraordinary but widely circulated theory of all is that the priest discovered that Christ's crucifixion was a clever fake and the Catholic Church bought his silence. Several books have been written about this most controversial theory.

In them, it is supposed that the altar documents traced the family tree of an old French royal dynasty, establishing direct descent from Christ. They claim that, contrary to Christian belief, Jesus was married to Mary Magdalen and they had children who married into European royalty. Far from being a poor carpenter, Jesus, so the theory goes, was in reality an aristocrat and his miracles were simple magician's tricks. His crucifixion, ordered by the Romans who were worried about his popularity, was faked. After sniffing opium on the cross, he was knocked out and appeared to be dead, enabling him to 'rise from the dead' after being placed in the tomb.

Christ supposedly lived on in the Holy Land for another 40 years. But Mary, Christ's children and several relatives took a ship to France. They landed at Marseilles and settled in Rennes le Chateau. There the children met and married into the French nobility, principally the Merovingian dynasty, which was based around Rennes.

Sauniere, it has been suggested, showed his newly discovered family tree to the wealthy descendants 2000 years on. They paid him millions to find out more and to keep his mouth shut until they could claim their lineage unchallenged. It is also said that the Vatican gave him money rather than allow the Bible story to be exposed as a fake.

This weird theory has been developed further by some researchers into the priest's secret. They claim that Christ's body was actually brought to France and buried, together with his treasure and documentary evidence, beneath the so-called eternal spring in the nearby area known as the Vale Of God.

A totally different theory for the priest's wealth is that the documents and maps led him to buried treasure. Nearly 2000 years ago the area of Rennes le Chateau was the royal treasury of the Visigoths, a Teutonic army that swept down from central Europe and ransacked Italy's palaces. It is a historic fact that Visigoth treasure was buried in the Vale Of God. This peaceful valley is three miles from Rennes le Chateau and it is believed that the two are linked by secret tunnels. The priest and his housekeeper Marie used to go for long walks into the countryside and return lugging heavy bags.

Marcel Captier, whose great grandfather was the priest's bellringer, says: 'There has always been suspicion that Sauniere's wealth was linked to the Vale Of God.' Captier, who still lives in Rennes, adds: 'There are many theories about what it was Sauniere found but they're all riddled with holes. The truth is that no one knows.'

Of the fake crucifixion theory, Marcel Captier says: 'Why should Christ's apparent descendants want to keep such a proud claim quiet? Why wouldn't they investigate it themselves rather than leave it to Sauniere, a parish priest with no apparent resources? Why should the Vatican accept that the family tree was anything but a mediaeval forgery? And why should so many important people allow themselves to be blackmailed by a simple country priest? Despite all the books written about Rennes le Chateau, no one has ever proved any of these theories.'

Englishwoman Celia Brooke, who now looks after St Mary Madgdalen Church in Rennes, raises new suspicions about the priest's wealth. She says: 'Behind the altar there is a room where Sauniere used to lock himself away after services. No one would ever see Sauniere leave it, yet he would be spotted later on carrying heavy sacks. We have found a hidden passageway out of the church from this room. I believe he used it to make his way down to the Vale Of God, probably by tunnels.'

The theory doesn't explain why Sauniere's deathbed confession was so horrifying that he was refused the last rites. Celia Brooke says: 'I have been here a quarter of a century and I don't know the answer. I don't think we ever will.'

Another Englishwoman living in the area is Patricia Logan, who left her home in York in 1982 to settle in the Vale Of God. At the time, she had no idea of stories that the world's most fabulous fortune could be buried in or around her back garden.

The eternal spring that bubbles out of the rich red soil has been pinpointed by some researchers as the hiding place for ancient treasure looted by the Visigoths from all over Europe and the Holy Land. A solid wall was built over the spring before the water was diverted some 200 years ago. Patricia says: 'I can't wait for the wall to crumble so I can dig beneath the foundations. But I won't let bulldozers spoil the countryside.'

Patricia, who runs a holiday home in the valley, says the alternative theory about Sauniere's wealth is even more intriguing to her. She says: 'I might be standing on Christ's tomb. If this is his last resting place, it makes the priest's grave robbery all the more horrifying and could explain why he was refused the last rites.'

Local farmer Francois Sauzede has the last word. Tapping his stick in the sunbaked soil, he says: 'I have known since I was child that the key to power, riches and fame is buried here. That is knowledge that my father and grandfather gave me. Everyone else in the village was brought up knowing it too. But just try finding out where or even what that secret is . . .'

Tutankhamun

On 17 February 1923 an archaeologist mumbled a phrase that has since echoed through the years, as the final wall of the sealed, boy-king's tomb was breached – and a curse too sinister, too mysterious and too lethal for the modern world to comprehend was unleashed. When Howard Carter whispered breathlessly that he could see 'things, wonderful things' as he gazed in awe at the treasures of Tutankhamun, he and his compatriots were completely innocent of the terrible dark force they had released from the boy-king's 3000-year-old burial chamber.

The final blow of the excavators' pick had set free the Curse of the Pharaoh.

As Carter, together with fanatical Egyptologist Lord Carnarvon, looked at the treasures of gold, gems, precious stones and other priceless relics, they ignored the dire warning written all those centuries ago to ward off grave robbers. In the ancient hieroglyphics above their heads, it read: 'Death will come to those who disturb the sleep of the pharaohs.'

For Carter and Lord Carnarvon, who had financed the dig culminating in history's greatest archaeological find, all thoughts of curses and hocus-pocus were forgotten as they revelled in the joy of the victorious end to the dig. The site of Luxor had escaped the attentions of grave robbers down through the centuries, and consequently the treasure-packed tomb was a find beyond compare.

Lord Carnarvon, lost as he was in the magnificence of the moment, had not taken lightly the threats of the ancient Egyptian high priests. In England, before the expedition had begun, he had consulted a famous mystic of the day, Count Hamon, who warned him: 'Lord Carnarvon do not enter tomb. Disobey at peril. If ignored will suffer sickness. Not recover. Death will claim him in Egypt.' Two separate visits to mediums in England had also prophesied his impending doom.

However, armed with intelligence which promised to reveal the secret of the boy pharaoh's tomb and the treasures within, he vowed to carry on with the search. The accolades of the world's academics rained down on him and his team. The praise of museums and seats of learning as far apart as Cairo and California was heaped on them. Carnarvon revelled in the glittering prize of fame – little knowing that he had but two months to enjoy the fruits of his success.

On 5 April 1923, just 47 days after breaching the chamber into Tutankhamun's resting place,

The beaten-gold, bejewelled funeral mask of the
legendary boy-king, Tutankhamun.

Carnarvon died in agony – the victim, apparently, of an infected mosquito bite.

At the moment of his death in the Continental Hotel, Cairo, the lights in the city went out in unison, and stayed off for some minutes. And if further proof were needed that it was indeed a strange force that was at work, thousands of miles away in England, at Lord Carnarvon's country house, his dog began baying and howling – a blood-curdling, unnatural lament which shocked the domestic staff deep in the middle of the night. It continued until one last whine, when the tormented creature turned over and died.

Could this be the work of the curse, the untapped source of evil which Carnarvon and Carter had unleashed? Certainly the newspapers of the day began to draw the sensational conclusion that it was – especially when, 2 days after Carnarvon's death at the age of 57, the mummified body of the pharaoh was examined and a blemish was found on his left cheek exactly in the position of the mosquito bite on Carnarvon's face.

Perhaps this could have been passed off as coincidence had it not been for the bizarre chain of deaths that were to follow. Shortly after Carnarvon's demise, another archaeologist, Arthur Mace, a leading member of the expedition, went into a coma at the Hotel

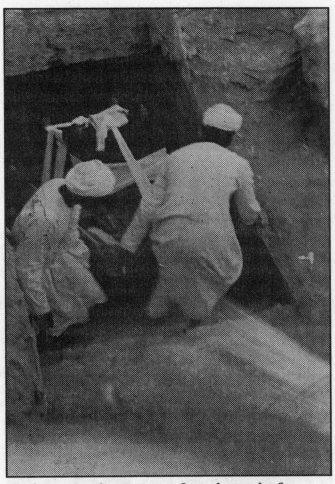

Workers removing treasures from the tomb of Tutankhamun – is there any truth to the legend that they incurred the wrath of the gods?

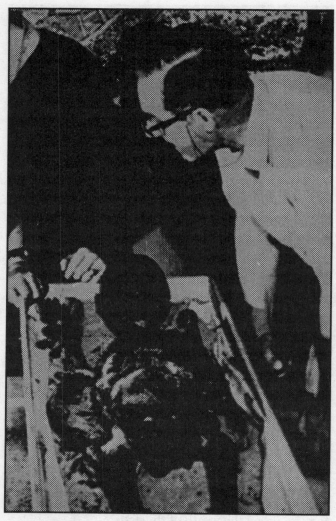

Egypt, 1968. The coffin of Tutankhamun is opened for only the second time this century.

Continental after complaining of tiredness. He died soon afterwards, leaving the expedition medic and local doctors baffled.

The deaths continued. A close friend of Carnarvon, George Gould, made the voyage to Egypt when he learned of his fate. Before leaving the port to travel to Cairo he looked in at the tomb. The following day he collapsed with a high fever; twelve hours later he was dead.

Radiologist Archibald Reid, a man who used the latest X-ray techniques to determine the age and possible cause of death of Tutankhamun, was sent back to England after complaining of exhaustion. He died soon after landing.

Carnarvon's personal secretary, Richard Bethell, was found dead in bed from heart failure four months after the discovery of the tomb.

The casualties continued to mount. Joel Wool, a leading British industrialist of the time, visited the site and was dead a few months later from a fever which doctors could not comprehend.

Six years after the discovery, twelve of those present when the tomb was opened were dead. Within a further seven years only two of the original team of excavators were still alive. Lord Carnarvon's half-brother apparently took his own life while temporarily insane, and a further 21 people connected in some way with the dig, were also dead. Of the original pioneers of the excavation, only Howard Carter lived to a ripe old age, dying in 1939 from natural causes.

Over the years, countless Egyptologists and academics have tried to probe the basis of the legend of the curse in a bid to debunk it as a myth. Others have tried to explain it – perhaps the strangest theory being advanced by atomic scientist Louis Bulgarini. In 1949 he wrote:

'It is definitely possible that the ancient Egyptians use atomic radiation to protect their holy places. The floors of the tombs could have been covered with uranium. Or the graves could have been finished with radioactive rock. Rock containing both gold and uranium was mined in Egypt. Such radiation could kill a man today.'

Professor Bulgarini's comfortable hypothesis does not explain the other victims of the curse. Men like Mohammed Ibrahim, Egypt's director of antiquities, who in 1966 argued with the government against letting the treasures from the tomb leave Egypt for an exhibition in Paris. He pleaded with them to allow the relics to stay in Cairo because he had suffered terrible nightmares of what would happen to him if they left the country. Ibrahim left a final meeting with the government officials, stepped out into what looked like a clear road on a bright sunny day, was hit by a car and died instantly.

Perhaps even more bizarre was the case of

Richard Adamson who by 1969 was the sole surviving member of the 1923 expedition. Adamson had lost his wife within 24 hours of speaking out against the curse. His son broke his back in an plane crash when he spoke out again.

Still sceptical, Adamson, who had worked as a security guard for Lord Carnarvon, defied the curse and gave an interview on British television, in which he still said that he did not believe in the curse. Later that evening, as he left the television studios, he was thrown from his taxi when it crashed, a swerving lorry missed his head by inches, and he was put in hospital with fractures and bruises. It was only then that the stoic Mr Adamson, then aged 70, was forced to admit: 'Until now I refused to believe that my family's misfortunes had anything to do with the curse. But now I am not so sure.'

Perhaps the most amazing manifestation of the curse came in 1972, when the treasures of the tomb were transported to London for a prestigious exhibition at the British Museum. Victim number one was Dr Gamal Mehrez, Ibrahim's successor in Cairo as director of antiquities. He scoffed at the legend, saying that his whole life had been spent in Egyptology and that all the deaths and misfortune through the decades had been the result of pure coincidence. He died the night after supervising the packaging of the relics for transport to England by a Royal Air Force plane.

The crew members of that aircraft suffered death, injury, misfortune and disaster in the years that followed their cursed flight.

Flight Lieutenant Rick Laurie died in 1976 from a heart attack. His wife declared: 'It's the curse of Tutankhamun – the curse has killed him.' Ken Parkinson, Flight Engineer, suffered a heart attack each year at the same time as the flight aboard the Britannia aircraft which brought the treasures to England until a final fatal one in 1978. Before their mission to Egypt neither of the servicemen had suffered any heart trouble, and had been pronounced fit by military doctors.

During the flight, Chief Technical Officer Ian Lansdown kicked the crate that contained the death mask of the boy king. 'I've just kicked the most expensive thing in the world,' he quipped. Later, on disembarking from the aircraft on another mission, a ladder mysteriously broke beneath him and the leg he had kicked the crate with was badly broken. It was in plaster for nearly six months.

Flight Lieutenant Jim Webb who was aboard the aircraft lost everything he owned after a fire devastated his home. A steward, Brian Rounsfall, confessed to playing cards on the sarcophagus of Tutankhamun on the flight home and suffered two heart attacks. And a woman officer on board the plane was forced to leave the RAF after having a serious operation.

The mystery remains. Were all those poor souls down the years merely the victims of some gigantic set of coincidences? Or did the priestly guardians of the tomb's dark secrets really exert supernatural forces which heaped so much misery and suffering on those who invaded their sacred chambers – and exact a terrible punishment on the despoilers of the magnificent graves of their noble dead?

Nessie

They call her a monster – but no one ever thinks of her as such. Of all the mysterious creatures that waft through the skies, creep across the earth or lurk in the depths, Nessie scares no one! She is everyone's favourite, this lady of the lake, this gentle giant of Loch Ness.

Locals around the Invernesshire lake have known for centuries about their mysterious neighbour, which they have always referred to in Gaelic as a 'water horse' rather than a monster. As children, they were warned not to swim in Loch Ness because of the 'kelpie'. But it was only in the 1930s, when a new road was being cut into the rocky north shore of the lake, that outsiders began to take notice of Nessie.

A gang of workman engaged on blasting operations in the summer of 1933 were startled to see Nessie, with 'an enormous head and broad body', speeding up the centre of the lake in the wake of a fishing boat. Another three witnesses spoke of 'several humps' rising and falling across the perfectly calm lake in an undulating motion 'rather like the movement of a caterpillar'.

The most detailed sighting of 1933, however, and the one that really gave birth to the worldwide legend of the Loch Ness monster, was

A snapshot taken in 1934 purported to show the Loch Ness monster.

Could this be Nessie? The debate still rages.

recounted by Mrs John Mackay. She was being driven by her husband along the new road which, now that trees and undergrowth had been cut down, gave a perfect view of the vast lake. 'I couldn't believe what we were seeing,' she said. 'I had never seen such an enormous thing. It was just an enormous black body, going up and down. You could not put a name to it. It could have been an elephant or a whale.'

That same year, Mr E.G. Boulenger, director of the aquarium at London Zoo, said that reports of Nessie were 'a striking example of mass hallucination'. He claimed that once Nessie was seen by a few people, she would be reported by many more.

He was correct – but only in that sightings came thick and fast in the following years. Over 3000 claims have been taken seriously by experts since Boulenger's dismissive words – from that of a ship's captain and crew to that of a vicar's tea party guests and even to that of a saint!

For the first sightings of Nessie predate the 1933 publicity by thousands of years. In AD 565 St Columba was travelling through Scotland's Great Glen converting the Picts and Scots to Christianity. He came to Loch Ness, where he found local people recovering the body of a neighbour who had been savaged by a monster while out swimming. One of the saint's followers swam out into the loch to retrieve a boat when he, too, was confronted by the beast. According to the then Abbot of Ionna, who wrote St Columba's biography, 'A strange beast rose from the water something like a frog, only it was not a frog.' St Columba ordered the monster: 'Go no further, nor touch that man.' Meekly, the predator turned on his tail and fled.

That was the beginning of the legend of the Loch Ness monster, a legend kept alive over the centuries through Scottish folklore which tells of kelpies (malignant water sprites) disguising themselves as horses in order to lure and kill human victims. In Gaelic, the monster was known as 'Niseag'.

The Victorians' favourite novelist, Sir Walter Scott, was obviously familiar with the stories. He wrote in his journal in 1827: 'Clan Ronald told us that a set of his kinsmen, believing that the fabulous water cow inhabited a small lake near his house, resolved to drag the monster into day. With this in view, they bivouacked by the side of the lake in which they placed, by way of nightbait, two small anchors such as belong to boats, each baited with the carcass of a dog slain for the purpose. They expected the water cow would gorge on the bait and were prepared to drag her ashore the next morning.' Happily, Nessie did not take the bait!

There have been many who have believed that Nessie and her breed can live on land as well as water. Margaret Cameron told of her youthful experience during World War I when she heard 'crackling' in the trees and saw a creature slither down into the water. She said that it had a shiny skin the colour of an elephant and two short round feet at the front. 'It had a huge body,' she said, 'and its movement was like a caterpillar.'

Farmer Jock Forbes and his companion had a similar experience in 1919. The pony pulling their trap suddenly reared up at the sight of a beast in their path. 'It came out of the trees, moved slowly across the road and then went down the bank,' he said. 'I heard a splash as, presumably, it went into the water.' Jock estimated that the beast was as long as the road was wide.

In 1923 chauffeur Alfred Cruickshank described his sighting of a monster he encountered on a country road: 'It had a large humped body standing about six feet high with its belly trailing on the ground. Its belly was about twelve feet long to which was attached a long thick tale about twelve feet in length. It was moving slowly, sort of waddling on two legs.'

Tourist George Spicer, from London, described the monster in 1933 as a 'loathsome sight' – a huge snail with a long neck and carrying what looked like a dead lamb in its mouth. He said: 'It did not move in the usual reptilian fashion but with a sort of arched walk. The body shot across the road in jerks. The body was about five feet in height and filled the road. Its colour could be called elephant grey.'

More usual are sightings of the Loch Ness monster in her own watery environment. In 1938 a tug captain and his mate noticed a huge, black 'animal with seven humps' emerge from the depths of Loch Ness and swim alongside their vessel before accelerating away 'at terrific speed', leaving large waves.

Forestry worker Lachlan Stuart, who lives on the lochside, told in 1951 how he had got up early to milk his cow when he saw humps speeding along the middle of the lake. He immediately thought that it was Nessie 'which has been seen several times in this vicinity this week'. He said that the monster swung towards him and swam within ten feet of the shore. He was so frightened, he said, that he retreated into trees before Nessie turned with a great splashing and vanished.

In 1960 the Rev W.L. Dobb had just finished a lakeside picnic with his family and guests when their attention was diverted by mysterious waves moving across the loch. Then a large hump broke the surface; a second hump followed, rising and falling as they moved down the loch.

In 1974 truck driver Andy Call and his mate Henry Wilson saw foaming water as they drove along the side of the loch. A creature surfaced. Call later said: 'It was black, 50 or 60 feet long, with a horse-like head. We watched it for fifteen minutes. It submerged three times.'

Lorry driver Hugh Chisholm had told his wife Mhairi that he had seen Nessie but she did not believe him. However, in 1978 both of them were driving along the loch and spotted the monster. 'It was really huge,' they said, 'with the head and one hump clearly visible. When it vanished under the water it left large waves behind.'

It sometimes seems as if Nessie has been playing a tantalising game of hide-and-seek with the human race over the centuries. Certainly Loch Ness is the right place to hide if you're a monster seeking her privacy. For the lake is deep and dark.

Loch Ness, a slash across the map of Scotland, is the result of a giant tear in the Earth's surface, gouged out 10,000 years ago by the last of the Ice Age glaciers. The lake is 1000 feet deep, 24 miles long, with water blackened by the peaty rivers that flow into it. So cold is it that bodies of drowned men never return to the surface.

The loch itself does present problems in investigating the Nessie legend because of its situation. It can play tricks on the eyes. It is a large mass of water sometimes completely calm in a way that the sea rarely is and its high shoreline casts deep shadows and reflections. Sceptics of the legend say that sightings can usually be put down to the wake of passing vessels, ripples caused by wind changes or simply logs floating in the water. The sheer volume of eyewitness evidence, however, has made many scientists sit up and take serious notice.

They recognise that it is not possible for all the witnesses to be either drunks, liars or just plain mistaken.

Two of the strongest pieces of evidence to support the existence of Nessie were put to stringent scientific analysis. They were two cine films, far more difficult to fake than still photographs, and were submitted to the Joint Air Reconnaissance Intelligence Centre by David James of the Loch Ness Investigation Bureau. The first, shot by Tim Dinsdale, shows a hump moving slowly away from the camera then speeding sideways across the field of vision before submerging. The analysts said the object was nearly five-and-a-half feet wide and moved at about ten miles per hour. And, they added, it was 'probably animate'.

The second film was taken by Mr Richard Raynor during a Loch Ness Expedition in 1967. It clearly shows an animal speeding through the water, then submerging when a boat enters its vision. Raynor was prepared to accept that it was an otter – but the reconnaissance experts said that it could have been seven feet long, far too long for such a creature.

Scientists next turned to echo sounders and sonar to establish the truth. The systems rely on sound waves being deflected by underwater objects. The shape of the rebounds can be refined to a stage where a picture can be drawn. Various expeditions between 1962 and 1977 claimed they found positive proof of an extraordinary being in the loch. Experiments indicated an animate contact larger than a salmon, moving in a manner not normally associated with a fish. But they could go no further than that.

Perhaps the most ambitious studies ever into the Loch Ness phenomenon were the expeditions launched in 1970 and 1975 by Dr Robert Rines, president of the Academy of Applied Science in Belmont, Massachusetts. Using underwater photography for the first time as a serious investigative aid, Rines equipped his team with strobe lighting, a time-lapse camera – and a 'sex cocktail' made from the essences of sea cows, eels and sealions to attract Nessie into camera range.

The scientist said: 'We wouldn't have been here if we didn't have the suspicion that there is something very large in this loch. My own view, after having personal interviews with highly reliable people, is that there is an amazing scientific discovery awaiting the world in Loch Ness.'

The world had to continue waiting. For the result of Rines's efforts was one spectacular picture which was claimed to be the upper torso, neck and head of a lake creature. The scientific world found the Rines report inconclusive, to say the least, but renowned naturalist Sir Peter Scott, who had helped launch the Loch Ness Phenomena Investigation Bureau in 1962, was sufficiently impressed to announce: 'There are probably between 20 and 50 of them down there. I believe they are related to the plesiosaurs.'

Since the plesiosaur has not been seen on earth for 70 million years, Scott's theory meant that Nessie and her ancestors were cut off from the sea when the loch was formed at the end of the last Ice Age. Why then have no bodies or bones been found on the lake's banks over the centuries? Scientists argue that it is possible that the water pressure in the great depths would slow down decomposition and allow time for eels to dispose of the remains.

Is it feasible that such creatures from another age could have survived in a genuine time warp in the depths of Loch Ness?

New discoveries are made in every age. The Komodo dragon which inhabits the remoter islands of Indonesia, was only discovered this century. And the coelacanth, which was believed to have been extinct for 70 million years, was found alive and well in the Indian Ocean in 1938. We know that the giant monsters who lived on land died out because they could not adapt. But we do not know what happened to the species who were at home in the water.

However, all scientists agree on one thing: whatever is lurking in the depths of Loch Ness, if indeed there is anything, has never been seen on earth before. Fish, reptile, mammal or amphibian – Loch Ness is not giving up her secret lightly.

Glenn Miller

Glenn Miller was one of the best-loved musicians of this century. To a world ravaged by war, he brought a musical style which was both harmonious and fun. From New York to Northumberland, and Africa to Asia, the strains of *In The Mood*, *Moonlight Serenade* and *String of Pearls* could be heard in every dance hall. Music made Miller and his band rich and the people who listened to it happy. And Miller knew that when the World War II ended, he could step out of the uniform of a US Army captain and resume his life as a professional musician.

On 15 December 1944 Glenn Miller boarded an aeroplane at an airfield north of London and headed for Paris. He was never seen again.

No wreckage was found, no body, nothing. For his many loyal fans, the tragedy of his disappearance was compounded by the fact that there was no grave to his memory, no monument to turn into a shrine. To this day, exactly how Glenn Miller met his end remains a complete mystery.

Miller, aged 40 at the time, was travelling to the recently liberated French capital to prepare a Christmas concert for the British and American servicemen occupying the city. Normally his manager would have made the arrangements but

Glenn Miller, the King of Swing and popular orchestra leader of World War II, disappeared in 1944 while flying over the English Channel. Did his plane crash – or was he secretly murdered in Paris?

Miller, for unexplained reasons, decided to make the trip himself. The band, composed of Air Force personnel, was to follow him over later.

At Twinwoods airfield, Bedfordshire, Miller boarded a single-engine Norseman D-64 aircraft, renowned throughout the service for its reliability and sturdiness. There were fog warnings, but the pilot was completely confident that he could handle the weather conditions. On board were the pilot, Miller and another American officer. Nothing of them, or the aircraft, has ever been seen since. The theory most widely accepted at the time was that ice formed on the aircraft, the extra weight dragging it down towards the waters of the English Channel. All its occupants were presumed drowned.

Over the years, however, a whole host of strange, not to say disquieting theories have arisen. One man, John Edwards, became obsessed by the disappearance of the band leader and spent a small fortune in researching how he met his end. Edwards, a former RAF pilot, devoted two decades to trying to solve the riddle of the disappearance in an investigation that cost him about £10,000.

His theory is now one of the most contentious: that Miller, a well-known womaniser, was not killed as the result of a flying accident, but that he was murdered.

According to Edwards, Miller died ignominiously of a fractured skull in the Pigalle district of Paris, the notorious haunt of pimps and prostitutes, three days after the aircraft vanished. Edwards also claims to have spoken to a man who says he saw Miller switch planes shortly after the Norseman had taken off. For Edwards says the aircraft went only as far as an airfield at Bovingdon, Hertfordshire, where Miller switched to a Dakota transport plane, which then flew him on to Paris.

Bizarre? Certainly, but in the fog of war, when morale is everything, Edwards claims that there was an official cover-up of the true circumstances of Miller's death. Edwards says:

'Why was there no official full inquiry? I have met great difficulty in trying to solve this mystery. Records have been reported burned. Other information, like the air crew report, is unaccountably vague. Even the weather conditions were listed as unknown. But pieces of information I collected over the years eventually all fell into place. I have evidence that an American military doctor in Paris signed Miller's death certificate. A retired US Air Force lieutenant-colonel recalls being told by the Provost Marshall's police office in Paris that Miller had been murdered. And I know a man in Miller's band who stated that it was common knowledge to those close to him that his boss was murdered in Paris.'

Edwards is not the only one who believes that there was something suspicious about the last flight of the band leader. In 1978 a medium called Carmen Rogers held an eerie psychic session at the deserted Twinwoods airfield. She said:

'I could see him walking to the aircraft with two other men. Miller was disturbed and worried about his domestic and other affairs. He did not want to make the trip to Paris. He felt sick and afraid. After they took off Miller asked the pilot to land. The pilot put down as soon as possible and let Miller get out. The aircraft touched down on the Essex side of the Thames estuary. Then Miller got out and made a phone to call to London and arranged his own disappearance.'

Many other theories have been put forward, including those that he was a spy on a mission, or that he suffered from amnesia. Many wrecked aircraft have been found in the Channel, but never the skeleton of his plane – a fact which continues to fuel rumours about the mystery of that tragic flight.

The Bermuda Triangle

The five US Navy Avenger bombers climbed in tight formation into the cloudless skies above their base at Fort Lauderdale, Florida. Theirs was a routine mission. The crews had been briefed to perform practice bombing runs on some old wrecks dotted along the Chicken Shoals sandbank, north of the small island of Bimini.

Normally each aircraft had a complement of three but that afternoon, 5 December 1945, one of the airmen had been pulled off the assignment at his own request. It made no difference to the men who comprised Flight No 19.

The bombers started out on an easterly course, intending to travel 160 miles before turning north for 40 miles and then returning on a south-west track to Lauderdale. The first part of the mission went like clockwork, with the bombing runs completed in text-book fashion.

Then around an hour after take-off the voice of flight leader Lieutenant Charles Taylor, an experienced pilot and war veteran, crackled into the headphones of the Lauderdale controller.

'Calling tower. This is an emergency. We seem to be off course. We cannot see land. Repeat. We cannot see land.'

Controller: 'What is your position?'

Taylor: 'We are not sure of our exact position. We cannot be sure just where we are. We seem to be lost.'

The controller calmly advised Taylor to take the squadron due west. Provided they were somewhere off the Florida Coast this would inevitably bring them back to land. The reply he received though was baffling.

Taylor: 'We don't know which way is west. Everything is wrong – strange. We cannot be sure of any direction. Even the ocean doesn't look the way it should.'

Now Lauderdale Air Traffic Control was completely mystified. True, some of the pilots on the mission were rookies. But Taylor had been through the mill. Even if his plane had suffered a compass failure, it should have been a simple matter for him to fly by the position of the sun.

As news of the drama spread around the base, senior Naval commanders arrived in the radio room to try and lend a hand. It was obvious that something was now terribly wrong. Pilots were asking each other for directions and nobody seemed able to take a lead. When the static cleared sufficiently for Control to get a message to Taylor his response left them incredulous.

Taylor said he believed he was somewhere over the Florida Keys which, if true, was so far south of the original flight plan as to be almost impossible. Lauderdale responded by urging him to head north. Officers there could not understand why, in clear weather, he had failed to follow the most obvious course of action – flying with the afternoon sun on his left.

Soon after this exchange the controller lost radio contact with the bombers. But snatches of conversations between the crewmen occasionally faded in and out through a fuzz of static. From these snippets it seemed Lieutenant Taylor had decided he was unfit to lead the squadron and had passed command to another experienced officer, Captain Stiver.

But Stiver fared little better. At one point the air base heard him say: 'We are not sure where we are. We think we must be 225 miles south-east of base. We must have passed over Florida and be in the Gulf of Mexico.' Later he instructed his pilots to follow him in a 180° turn which he hoped would lead them towards the Florida coast.

The last words Lauderdale managed to distinguish were chillingly matter-of-fact: 'Entering white water. We are completely lost.' According to the calculations of the land-based naval commanders, Flight 19 had headed west out into the Atlantic Ocean – and oblivion.

A Martin Mariner flying boat carrying thirteen crew was scrambled and ordered to sweep a search area for signs of wreckage. A few minutes into the flight the Mariner's captain radioed back to say he was being buffeted by strong winds at 6000 feet. Then his plane vanished too. There was no distress call.

By now every available ship in the area had been alerted, including US submarines and destroyers and British frigates based on the Bahamas. None of them found any wreckage. Six planes had vanished and 27 men were missing presumed dead.

The legend of the Bermuda Triangle was born.

It was not until 16 May 1991 that the planes were found, just ten miles off the Florida coast, by a diving team hunting Spanish galleon wrecks. They were all within 2 miles of one another and lying in some 750 feet of water.

But if the discovery explained where the Avengers ditched, it could not explain why: why two experienced pilots, on different aircraft, suddenly found it impossible to navigate by the sun; why they reported the ocean looking 'strange'; and why if, as some experts have suggested, they were the victims of bizarre weather, they made no mention of this in communications with the Lauderdale base.

Unquestionably, the Bermuda Triangle lies in an area notorious for its treacherous seas, bizarre calms and sudden violent storms. Many writers have cited this alone as sufficient explanation for the 100 ships and aircraft known to have vanished within its borders, taking with them an estimated 1000 lives. Others cite the unpredictable and powerful currents of the Gulf Stream and the deep, uncharted trenches criss-crossing the sea bed.

It is also fair to say that over the years the legend has grown courtesy of some imaginative newspaper reporting. The original triangle as defined by US author Vincent Gaddis takes a line from Florida to Bermuda, from Bermuda to Puerto Rico and from Puerto Rico through the Bahamas to Florida. It is often stretched to accommodate the position of any ship which happens to sink in that part of the Atlantic. In fact, such loose reporting serves only to scramble the well documented accounts of genuine mysteries centring on the Triangle.

For although the mystery of Flight 19 gave the Bermuda Triangle its international infamy, it was by no means first to fall victim. As long ago as 1880 the British frigate *Atlanta* and its crew of 290 cadets vanished in the same area. Six vessels of the Royal Navy's Channel Fleet patrolled the waters for four months without finding so much as a fragment of wreckage.

Another baffling disappearance centres on the 300-plus crew of the *USS Cyclops*, a newly-built,

500 foot, 19,500-ton supply ship, which was carrying manganese ore between Barbados and Norfolk, Virginia. There was no distress call, the weather was calm and sunny and the *Cyclops* was equipped with brand new, thoroughly tested radio equipment.

Because World War I was in progress at the time of the tragedy, it was thought she must have been hit by a German mine or been torpedoed. This theory held until a later study of Germany's war records showed that there was no minefield and no naval aggressor in the area at the time.

After the Flight 19 fiasco, the list of disappearances began to grow almost by the month.

There was the British airliner *Star Tiger*, a four-engined Tudor-Four, which in 1948 informed its Bermuda controller that it expected to arrive on schedule. The aircraft was 400 miles north-east of Bermuda at the time. Neither the plane nor its 31 passengers and crew were ever found.

There was the private charter DC3 which, in the same year, headed towards Miami airport insisting: 'We are approaching the field. All's well.' Not a trace of its wreckage was ever found.

And there was the disappearance in 1963 of two brand new US Air Force KC135 Stratotankers from Homestead air base, Florida. They were lost while flying to a refuelling rendezvous 300 miles south-west of Bermuda.

So what explanation – apart from the questionable freak weather theory – can explain such massive loss of life in such a comparatively small sea area.

One theory centres on the fact that the Bermuda Triangle is one of only two places in the world in which a compass points to true, rather than magnetic, North. The other location is the equally dangerous Devil's Sea, south-east of Japan. This quirk of nature is thought to confuse fish to the point where they have even been seen swimming upside down. Yet it could not surely be enough to explain the catalogue of catastrophes in the Triangle.

Other suggestions are even more bizarre. That aliens have established an underwater citadel in which they carry out research on the ships and planes they capture. That the lost civilisation of Atlantis is carrying out a similar trick. That horrific whirlpools spin out of nowhere to suck ships and planes to their deaths.

The truth is perhaps best summed up in a report produced for the United States' National Oceanic and Atmospheric Administration.

'Despite efforts by the Unites States Air Force, Navy and Coast Guard,' it concluded, 'no reasonable explanation to date has been found for the vanishments.'

Serpents

Does Nessie have a cousin? Or an entire family of relations scattered around a distant continent? As many as 100 lakes and rivers in North America have been credited with being haunted by underwater monsters.

Judge this evidence from Mr Richard Miller, editor of the *Vernon Advertiser*, on the subject of the mysterious resident of Lake Okanagan, near the United States border in British Columbia. Miller was visiting the lake with his wife in July 1959 when he saw what he believed was the creature the locals know as 'Ogopogo'. He reported in his newspaper:

'Returning from a cruise down the Okanagan Lake, travelling at ten miles an hour, I noticed, about 250 feet in our wake what appeared to be the serpent. On picking up the field glasses my thoughts were verified. It was Ogopogo and it was travelling a great deal faster than we were. I would judge around fifteen to seventeen miles an hour. The head was about nine inches above the water. The head was definitely snake-like with a blunt nose.'

'Our excitement was short-lived. We watched for about three minutes. As Ogie did not appear to like the boat coming on him broadside, he very gradually reduced the five humps which were so plainly visible, lowered his head and gradually submerged. At no time was the tail visible. The family's version of the colour is very dark greenish. This sea-serpent glides gracefully in a smooth motion (without snake-like undulations sideways. This would lead one to believe that in between the humps it possibly has some sort of fin which it works together or possibly individually to control direction.'

The Miller family's spectacular sighting was far from being the first of Ogopogo. In fact, verifiable sightings were being recorded long before the Loch Ness monster's notoriety. Its home is about the same depth as Loch Ness but much longer (80 miles) and much colder. First reports of the great Ogopogo came from Indians in the seventeenth century who described a huge, dark serpent with long neck and humped back. In Indian legend the creature was a murderer who had been changed into a water serpent in punishment for his crimes; hence the name Ogopogo, which means 'remorseful one'.

In 1875 Susan Allison saw what she had at first believed to be a log suddenly swim up the lake against the wind. In 1890 Captain Thomas Shorts was sailing across the lake when he saw an animal about fifteen feet long with a ram-like head and the sun shining through its fins.

In 1914 the rotting carcass of a strange animal was found washed up on a beach. It was five feet long with a round head, flippers and a broad tail, was blue-grey in colour and weighed two hundredweight. It was identified as a sea cow – but it was a long way from its natural habitat!

There were regular sightings throughout this century, but none so detailed and authoritative as that of the editor Miller.

Then, nine years later, came incredible cine film support for the monster theory. Sawmill worker Arthur Folden was driving with his wife on a clear day in August 1968 when they spotted a large object moving through the calm water of the lake. Folden stopped the car, took out his 8mm cine camera and for a minute filmed the creature swimming about 200 yards from the shore. Comparing the object to pine trees in the background, the creature must have been about 60 feet long.

Further cinematic evidence was produced in 1976 when Ed Fletcher and his daughter Diane were boating on the lake. Suddenly a creature cut across his bow and, as Fletcher related: 'If I hadn't shut the engine off I could have run him over – or jumped on his back. The boat drifted to within 30 feet of him.'

Father and daughter sped back to shore to pick up a camera and a further passenger to bear witness to the scene that ensued as Ogopogo appeared from the depths again and paraded before them for a full hour.

Fletcher said: 'I saw his whole length this time, about 70 to 75 feet. I shut the engine off when we got near him and the boat coasted to within 50 feet of him when I shot the first picture. He would submerge, swim at least two city blocks, then surface and all the while we chased him.'

Fletcher, who took five photographs of the creature, said that it swam coiled up and then stretched out. Diane Fletcher described it as 'turning like a corkscrew' and said its skin was smooth and brownish like that of a whale, with ridges on its back. The third witness said it had 'two things standing up from the head like the ears of a doberman pinscher'.

The photographs do show a humped object moving through the water. Sceptics argued that it could be a series of waves travelling in different directions and hitting each other – but that does not explain the monster's head.

New reports came thick and fast. And Ogie-hunting became as popular as trying to get Loch Ness to give up its similar secrets. Between April 1977 and August 1978 newspapers around Lake Okanagan carried a dozen reports.

Harry Staines, of Westbank, said: 'I did not believe it before but we circled the thing in our boat, keeping it about a hundred yards away.' He described it as long black eel about eleven metres long swimming with an undulating motion.

In 1977 sixty scuba divers took turns to be lowered into the lake in a reinforced cage. Armed with cameras and aircraft landing lights they waited nine metres down for Ogie to show up. But he failed to make the date.

The Federation of British Columbia Naturalists describes the reports as 'an optical illusion produced when an observer views obliquely a bow wave moving across flat water under certain lighting conditions'. But other respectable scientists feel that there is some type of primitive whale that lives in the Canadian river and lake network. Certainly sightings have come thick and fast from the area.

Creatures called Manipogos are said to lurk in the two lakes of Manitoba and Winnipegosis. Again the subject of early Indian legend, the beasts were first reported by white men in 1935. Most descriptions give the Manipogo a flat, snake-like head, dark skin and three humps. Some reports even gave it a mate and off-spring.

Sitting at a picnic table with his wife and two sons, Steve Rahaluk of Rorkton, Manitoba, saw a ripple in the water. 'When I first looked there was only one. But when I ran to the shore I could see another beside it and a third trailing behind.'

In 1962 news commentator Richard Vincent was out in a fishing boat when he spotted a large black snake about four yards long. Despite having an outboard motor they could not keep up with 'the monster'.

Dr James A. Macleod, chairman of the Zoological Department of the University of Manitoba, seriously investigated the possibility that some prehistoric reptile did survive in the northern end of the lake. In the 1930s a bone was found on the bed of Lake Manitoba but it was lost in a fire. A wooden replica was made which resembles a spinal vertebra 15 cm long and 7 cm wide. Macleod thought it was a bone from a long-extinct animal. However, other Manitoba University professors suggested that under certain climatic conditions – cold water with warm air – mirages can occur on lakes in the area.

Another waterway that straddles the Canadian-American border is Lake Champlain, also famous for its monster sightings. The aptly named 'Champ' was first spotted in 1609 by Samuel de Champlain, after whom the lake was named, who said it looked like a twenty foot snake with a horse's head.

The first reliable reports came after 1819 when the first settlers saw the creature in Bulwagge Bay. In 1871 passengers on the steamer *Curlew* described a monster with a head raised on an erect neck, leaving a wake 30 to 40 feet long. Showman Phineas T. Barnum offered a reward of $50,000 dollars for the skin of the sea serpent, which had to be delivered to New York in a copper boiler. There were no takers.

Seven years later, however, a Dr Brigham and Mr Ashley Shelters spotted the beast in Missiquoi Bay. They reported that its body was over twenty feet in length, that its head was as large as a flour barrel and it had eyes 'of greenish tinge'. Another supposedly reliable witness, Captain Mooney, sheriff of Clinton County, said that when he saw Champ its head was raised four or five feet out of the rough water.

Anything up to 100 lakes and rivers in North America have been sites of lake monster hauntings – from Arizona to the frozen wastes of northern Canada, and from the superstitious 1800s to the sceptical present day.

For instance, in 1883 a Utah journalist wrote about Bear Lake: 'There is abundant testimony on record of the actual existence at the present day of an immense animal – some species as yet unknown to science.' And in 1885 the captain of the steamer *US Grant* on Flathead Lake, Montana, wrote in his log that one of his passengers fired on a large whale-like animal.

A lake monster named Igopogo is still supposed to inhabit Simcoe Lake, Ontario. A minister, an undertaker and their families saw the creature in 1963 and described it as 'charcoal-coloured, 30 to 70 feet long and with dorsal fins'. Others have described it as 'dog-faced with a neck like a drain-pipe'.

One of the most romantic mysteries, however, was related in the late 1940s by a Canadian writer who told of a monster called Angeoa which was seen in Dubawnt Lake in the far north of the country. The bones of a great beast had once been found of the shore of the lake, which has the Eskimo name of Lake of the Heaped-up Bones. The author, Farley Mower, was told by an Eskimo friend: 'My father was with another man when he saw it. He said it was as long as twenty kayaks and broader than five. It had a fin which stood up from one end and that fin was as big as a tent.' Terrified, the two Eskimos fled from the creature but their kayak overturned and only the informant's father survived.

Sightings are still common on the giant Iliamna Lake in Alaska. NASA astronauts flying in a plane over the lake saw giant shadows moving in the water. When they swooped down to investigate, the shadows moved on. Science and legend came together when NASA investigated the sighting. An old Indian told the investigators how he saw someone shrivel up and die after seeing the lake monster . . .

Elvis

Every day, devoted fans of Elvis Aaron Presley file past his grave in solemn tribute to the pop legend they call 'The King'.

No singer, before or since, has inspired the kind of loyalty that brings hundreds of thousands of fans flocking to the 'sacred' site in the gardens of Elvis's home: Gracelands, Memphis, Tennessee.

For many of the faithful the pilgrimage is not made in grief but in wonder. They wallow in a mystery that, despite all the official evidence, remains among the most enduring of the twentieth century: Is Elvis really dead?

'No question,' says the Memphis coroner's office. 'He died on 16 August 1977, in the bathroom of his home at Gracelands.'

Certainly the pathologists at Baptist Memorial Hospital, Memphis, have no doubts. They found his body contained a lethal cocktail of drugs including codeine and Valium. There was enough codeine alone to kill – ten times the recommended dosage – and in total, traces of fourteen separate drugs were identified. The autopsy report states unequivocally: 'It is our view that the death in the case of Baptist Memorial Hospital A77-160 (Elvis Presley) resulted from multiple drug ingestion, commonly known as polypharmacy.'

A photograph of 'Elvis' taken by a fan at Gracelands on 1 January 1978, over four months after Elvis 'died'.

One of Elvis' last performances, given shortly before his 'death' in 1977.

There is little doubt that in his last months Elvis was a shambling parody of the star who once wowed the world's women with a flick of his hips. He was massively overweight, probably impotent and existed on a diet of junk food, booze and pills. When medics first saw his body, clad in gold pyjamas, his face was so discoloured that they believed the corpse was a black man.

He was buried inside two days, suspiciously quickly some fans argued later. Memphis medical examiner Dr Jerry Francisco announced that the singer had died of a heart attack, though the pathologists found no evidence to support this assertion. More worryingly, immediately after his death but before investigators arrived, someone cleaned the bathroom and removed all evidence of drug-taking.

Within a few days of Elvis's demise the first rumours had started. It was said that the 42-year-old star had faked his own death because he could no longer cope with the pressures of fame. Some suggested he had lain in a coffin under sedation to dupe mourners who had filed past paying their last respects. Some fans told of seeing mysterious beads of sweat on his face.

A second claim was that the body found was not Elvis, but that of a lookalike, which obviously implied the possibility of murder. If either conspiracy theory was true, there had to be an unprecedented collusion of police, doctors and government officials.

But what would be the motive for such collusion? Investigative journalist, Gail Brewer-Giorgio, believes she has a possible answer.

During his White House reign the late President Richard Nixon made Presley an official F.B.I. agent. At the time this was perceived as an honorary title in recognition of Elvis's interest in, and backing for, police work. But Brewer-Giorgio believes it meant much more. In her book *The Elvis Files* she suggests that he was working as an undercover agent in a huge anti-Mafia sting code-named 'Operation Fountain'.

To support this assertion Brewer-Giorgio cites the 30,000 pages of files on Elvis still retained by the F.B.I. Many of these refer to death threats against him while others are minutes of his secret meetings with Nixon. There are a further 600 files classified 'Top Secret' which will not be made public until well into the next century.

The mystery is deepened by the fact that the tax records of Elvis Aaron Presley, showing stocks and shares investments of $75 million, carry an F.B.I. registered social security number and a Red Flag mark, indicating that the contents are classified secret.

There are other strange coincidences surrounding Elvis's death. Not least are the payments made by Presley's company, Gracelands, to settle credit card bills run up by one Jon Burrows. Jon Burrows was an identity regularly used by Elvis when he wished to travel incognito. Up until 1991 the J. Burrows credit card seems to have been in active use.

Then there are the life insurance policies. Two of these, together worth around $2 million dollars, were cashed in before Elvis's death. The third – rumoured to be the most valuable – has never been claimed. Supporters of the conspiracy theory argue that this is because Elvis would never have countenanced fraud in staging his disappearance.

Other unanswered questions include the following:

Why did some of the star's most treasured personal possessions and mementoes, including family photographs, go missing after his death? It is hard to believe a burglar could have penetrated the intense Gracelands security net.

Why did trained graphologists risk ridicule by asserting that the writing on Elvis's death certificate was his own?

Why, two days before his death, did Elvis say formal farewells to his closest friends and staff?

Why was the star not buried, as he had asked, next to his mother in the family burial park? The plot reserved for him still lies empty.

In addition to all this, there are the dozens of Elvis sightings reported each year. Fans claim to have seen him in supermarkets, on beaches or walking down small town streets. There are even two photographs of a man said to be The King taken at Gracelands after his 'death'. One was taken through a glass door and shows him sitting in a chair. The other is a moody, brooding portrait of a man watching fans file past the Presley grave.

Critics accuse Brewer-Giorgio of exaggerating tabloid newspaper accounts in order to sensationalise her book. But there is other, independent evidence to suggest Elvis's death may not be quite all it seems.

In August 1991 one of the singer's oldest friends, pianist Gordon Stoker, received a typewritten letter purporting to be from Presley. It was delivered backstage during a charity concert at Tucson, Arizona. No one saw who dropped it off.

Stoker was leader of Presley's backing band *The Jordanaires*, and featured on many of the star's 170 big-selling hits. He was a constant ally during a career which saw Elvis sell a billion records, star in 33 films, perform 860 live shows and gross a personal fortune of $43 million (rising to $250 million after his death).

Stoker, of Nashville, Tennessee, is convinced

the letter is genuine because it carried the same spelling mistakes that Elvis always used to make. He argues that it would be impossible for a hoaxer to know such fine details.

'I now think that the person who was buried was not Elvis,' he said. 'I'm convinced that the letter is genuine. He said that he loved us all dearly and that he was always thinking of us.

'He also said: "I'm very sorry for having to do what I had to do. But I hope you understand."'

John Bradburne

In the poor, rural areas of Zimbabwe, the name of an Englishman called John Bradburne is synonymous with sainthood. Not just because of his selflessness in working with lepers, though that commitment was remarkable enough in itself. Rather, the case for beatifying Bradburne centres on the manner of his death, and the mysterious circumstances of his funeral. Many who were there that day are convinced they witnessed a miracle.

Bradburne was born, the son of a Norfolk country parson, in 1929. He saw wartime service as a Gurkha officer and after the fall of Singapore was forced into the Malayan jungle, an ordeal he survived through a combination of luck and quick wits. He emerged from the war mentally scarred by some of the horrors he had seen but also with the lifelong friendship of a fellow officer John Dove, later a Jesuit priest.

Back in civvy street Bradburne drifted into a few jobs, including forestry and teaching. His powerful faith combined with a growing restlessness eventually drove him into the arms of the church and he converted to Roman Catholicism in 1947. He flirted with becoming a monk, made a pilgrimage to Jerusalem and, while living in Southern Italy, made a commitment to celibacy in his prayers to the Virgin Mary. Those who knew the likeable, good-looking, well-spoken Englishmen believed he was desperately seeking an outlet for his faith, a life-mission to carry out God's work.

He found it shortly before his 40th birthday when John Dove, by now a priest in Rhodesia (as it was then known), invited him over to stay. Even then, Bradburne seemed unable to settle. It wasn't until 1969 when his friend Heather Benoy suggested they visit a leper camp at Mutemwa that his future became clear. He refused to return home to Salisbury (now Harare) and became the warden of this filthy, shambles of a settlement. He was to spend the rest of his life there.

Over the next ten years Bradburne introduced standards of care and hygeine that his crippled patients had never dreamed of. He cleared the rats that would gnaw their senseless limbs at night, cut the nails of those who still had fingers and toes and feed and bathe them. He wrote poems about each of the 80 patients under his care and when any were close to death he gave them inspirational strength by reading to them from the Bible. He also supervised the building of a small chapel in the settlement. Later he fell out with members of the Rhodesia Leprosy Association. They objected to his 'extravagance' at demanding one loaf of bread per leper per week. And they were appalled when he refused to place numbers around the necks of the lepers. 'These are men, not livestock,' he would tell them.

Bradburne was subsequently expelled from the settlement, but he refused to leave the area. He lived in a tin hut on a nearby mountain, often ministering to the lepers under cover of the night. With his long hair and beard, monk's habit (he had been granted the habit of a Third Order Franciscan) and emaciated figure, he was instantly recognisable.

By the summer of 1979 the civil war in Rhodesia was at its height. The main roads were kept open by the Government but in much of the countryside Patriotic Front guerillas were in the ascendancy. At midnight on 2 September a group of ten mujibha youths – the messengers and intelligence gathers of Robert Mugabe's army – called at John Bradburne's hut and kidnapped him. His friends believe he had been falsely denounced as a Rhodesian spy by a worker at Mutemwa, whom Bradburne had reprimanded for stealing rations reserved for lepers. Bradburne was taken to a meeting of hundreds of teenage mujibhas who mocked and abused him. They offered him excrement to eat, tried to make him dance to their music and offered him local girls to sleep with.

The following day the professional guerillas took over and moved Bradburne to a cave near the settlement of Gwaze. They were furious with the mujibhas for taking him from Mutemwa because their information was that he was a good man. But they were also worried about returning him. They feared he might reveal information about their hideout to the authorities.

During his interrogation he seemed oblivious to the questioning. At one point he knelt and prayed for ten minutes, infuriating the rebel commander. He rejected most of their food and when they suggested he could go and live in a neutral country like China (Mugabe's chief ally), he laughed out loud. Similarly he rejected an offer to work in Mozambique. 'I must return to the lepers at Mutemwa,' he told them.

That night Bradburne was marched towards the nearest main road where the guerilla commander ordered him to walk a few paces ahead. He was then told to turn and face the commander – but he fell on his knees and prayed, showing not a flicker of fear. When he rose to his feet the commander shot him.

The body was found the following morning by the only other white man still in the area, a Roman Catholic priest called Fr David Gibbs. Gibbs knew Bradburne well. He knew that the Englishman had once told a priest of his three greatest wishes: to serve and live with lepers, to die a martyr and to be buried in his Franciscan habit. Full of grief, Gibbs made a point of returning to Bradburne's hut to recover his habit for safe-keeping. But in all the drama that followed the murder, Gibbs forgot to dress the body in it. When he arrived at the funeral in Salisbury he placed Bradburne's habit on top of the coffin. It lay alongside three flowers which a friend of Bradburne had arranged there to symbolise his devotion to the Trinity – the Father, Son and Holy Ghost.

As the funeral progressed, the priest in charge noticed to his surprise that a drop of fresh blood had fallen from the coffin. He covered it with a cloth, but two more drops fell onto the material. The scene was witnessed by both Fr Gibbs and the local undertaker, who was horrified at his faulty workmanship. This was, after all, the funeral of a holy man.

After the ceremony the coffin was opened for inspection. There was no sign of any blood issuing from the body and the coffin walls were all clean and dry. Mouthing prayers, the undertaker and priests dressed Bradburne in his Franciscan habit, the last of his three wishes, and buried him.

Within weeks local people were speaking of him as a saint. The story of the three wishes, three flowers and three drops of blood took on the status of a supernatural mystery and many bizarre stories began to emerge. There was the woman who prayed to his memory and found herself cured of terminal cancer. And the man who claimed Bradburne had come to him in a dream to warn of the way his son would die. Others told how after talking to him or praying for him they were visited by swarms of bees or eagles, symbols of the Franciscan way of life.

John Bradburne prayer cards are now distributed across Zimbabwe. There is also a shrine to him at the leper colony which was his life work. But it may be many years before the Vatican confirms him as a saint. Material for his beatification, submitted to the Archbishop of Zimbabwe in 1986, was considered insufficient to make a final judgement.

Crop Circles

During the mid-1980s reports of a weird phenomena across rural England began to filter into the newspapers. Soon dozens of photographs appeared showing perfect circles of flattened crops clearly defined against the up-standing cereal around them.

There were no sign of any footprints, no damage outside the circle and, apparently, no motive. It was for all the world as though some alien spacecraft had hovered above the flattened area, left its mark and then zipped back into hyper-space. Which was exactly how the UFO lobby explained the whole, curious affair.

There were plenty of other theories though. Whirlwinds, hedgehogs, rabbits, the Devil, fairies, ancient earth power lines – all were volunteered as explanations. And then there were the hoaxes.

In the summer of 1991, with the corn circle debate raging across the country, two elderly British artists dropped a bombshell on the 'cerealogists'. Dave Chorley and Doug Bower claimed responsibility for all the main circles of the previous thirteen years. Their motive was to see how many so-called experts and New Age followers they could embarrass and fool. They

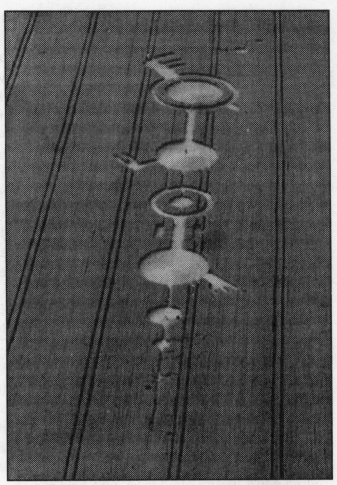

The work of aliens or hoaxers? A corn circle at Alton Barnes, Wiltshire.

were also intrigued to know how long the hoax would last.

Chorley and Bower claimed to have fooled the two leading British investigators, Colin Andrews and Pat Delgado, a team of Japanese scientists, farming groups and several government departments. They insisted that only poles, boards and ropes were necessary to construct a perfect circle.

The hoaxers told how they met in the late 1960s with a common interest in art and UFOs. A few years later, inspired by a famous 'flying saucer circle' in north-east Australia, they made their first attempt in Strawberry Field, near Cheesefoot Head, Winchester. These early circles attracted no media attention and the pair were soon on the brink of giving up. However their 1981 efforts at Cheesefoot Head were widely reported and their enthusiasm was re-kindled.

Whatever their claims, Chorley and Bower's pranks do not explain the crop circle phenomenon. It was always obvious to investigators that there were a lot of hoaxers around, and scientists conceded that distinguishing fact from fantasy was nigh on impossible. Parties of hoaxers with names such as 'Merlin & Co', the 'Bill Bailey Gang', the 'Wessex Sceptics' and 'Spiderman and Catwoman' ran rife in cornfields to the irritation of farmers. The average bill for crop damage was put at £60.

Farmers themselves were not entirely innocent. A surreptitious night's work and a phone call to the papers the next day often produced a queue of sightseers anxious for a close-up glimpse of one of the strange circles. There were stories of landowners charging a £2 admission fee plus £1 for parking.

The fact that a few country bumpkins managed to trick scientists and car-loads of gullible townies is one thing. To conclude from this that all crop circles are hoaxes is quite another. It is tantamount to saying that because art experts are often fooled by forgers, all old masters are fakes.

The plain fact is that there is nothing new about crop circles. They have manifested themselves in England for at least 4000 years. And while the modern day farmer is mostly able to shrug off crop damage, his Bronze Age counterpart, struggling to survive, may have taken a dim view. Any circle prankster living around 2000 BC could probably expect to get an axe through his head.

A study of the circles' history shows that in many cases the theories behind their creation have a strikingly familiar ring. Professor Plot, of Oxford University's Faculty of Science, and a fellow of the Royal Society, published a book called *The Natural History of Staffordshire* in

1686. In it he told of his desire to identify a 'higher principle' which might explain crop circles other than the then fashionable claims of rutting deer, over-active moles, urinating cattle and the fairies. One pamphlet published eight years earlier told of a field 'neatly mowed by the devil, or some infernal spirit'.

Plot did not dismiss these ideas but his own conclusion was that equally bizarre ball lightning was to blame. 'They must needs be the effects of lightning, exploded from the clouds most times in a circular manner,' he said. Today, the reality of ball lightning is only just gaining acceptance among mainstream scientists.

It is far from clear why there has been a 300 year gap in the study of crop circles. Perhaps it is because genuine cases are extremely rare. But for the labours of today's hoaxers the phenomena might never have been brought to the attention of a wider audience.

A study by Colin Andrews, carried out at a cost of £50,000 in 1983, concentrated on southern England. His twelve-strong team concluded that the circles were somehow linked to disturbances in the earth's magnetic field, which in turn stemmed from the hole in the ozone layer of the atmosphere. Sensors had picked up violent fluctuations in the force field around areas where a plethora of circles had appeared.

Mr Andrews, an electrical expert with his local council, reported: 'One of the circles that appeared recently in Hampshire amazed us even more than the others because the flattened crops grew back in dartboard formation. There were seven concentric rings of crops with a series of perfect spokes going out from the centre.'

The Andrews team even claimed that the molecular structure of the crops might have been damaged. Later, they returned to the fray asserting that circles were being created by 'some form of higher intelligence'. Andrews went on: 'They are caused by some sort of high energy, but we don't know what. The shapes are becoming more and more complex and I believe that what we are heading for is circles in the form of snowflakes or flowers. The shapes we have seen recently are just the start of what is to come.'

Throughout the 1980s reports of crop circles became even more widespread. Although southern England was still very much the epicentre, examples were found in Australia, North America and Japan. Scientists from these countries were soon clamouring for the chance to spend a summer in Britain to conduct in-depth scientific studies.

Amid all the outlandish theories, the most straightforward explanation continued to come from consultant meteorologist Dr Terence

Meaden, head of the Tornado and Storm Research Organisation. He reckoned unusual air vortices were a factor behind many circles. Such vortices occurred when a gust of wind on one side of a hill struck still air behind it.

'Some bone-headed people are trying to turn this whole thing into something spiritual or as a phenomenon from outer space,' he said. 'Basically, the circles are formed by a spiralling ball of air which comes down to the ground.'

Strong support for the Meaden theory came from a couple out walking along the edge of a corn field in the Hampshire countryside. It was a still August day in 1991, yet suddenly Gary and Vivienne Tomlinson, of Guildford, Surrey, saw the crops around them begin to move. They were caught in the middle of a forming circle.

Vivienne takes up the story: 'There was a tremendous noise. We looked up to see if it was caused by a helicopter but there was nothing. We felt a strong wind pushing us from the side and above. It was forcing down on our heads, yet incredibly my husband's hair was standing on end. Then the whirling air seemed to branch into two and zig-zag off into the distance. We could still see it like a light mist or fog, shimmering as it moved.'

'As it disappeared, we were left standing in a corn circle with the corn flattened all around us.

Everything became very still again and we were left with a tingly feeling. It all happened so quickly that it seemed to be over in a split second.'

Dr Meaden later interviewed the couple and was impressed by their power of recall. 'The story these people told is so detailed they cannot have made it up,' he said. 'They had no knowledge of corn circles yet they described a scientific process that could easily cause them. This really is a magnificent eye witness account – much better than any we have had previously.'

When the mystery is finally solved it will be hard to judge who is the more embarrassed. The 'experts' fooled by a few amateurs carrying planks and string. Or the hoaxers, who arrogantly believed it was all down to them.

Moa

Paddy Freaney stared with mounting incredulity at the enormous bird standing behind a bush some 40 yards away. Fully six feet tall, its body covered with reddish-grey feathers, the creature sported a long thin neck and small head. Freaney, SAS instructor turned hotelier, had never seen anything like it in his life.

Quickly he turned to the two men accompanying him on the hike through the Cragieburn mountains in New Zealand's South Island. High school teacher Sam Waby and gardener Rochelle Rafferty had been taking a drink from a river. As Freaney hissed an alert, they raced across to see why he was so excited.

Seconds later, Waby understood. 'Good God,' he breathed. 'It's a moa.'

All zoological wisdom held that the moa bird, in its larger form, had become extinct in the fifteenth century. A few peacock-sized versions of the flightless birds had managed to survive into the eighteenth century until they too were hunted out of existence. The species was exclusive to New Zealand.

Freaney managed to squeeze off a single, blurred photograph as the mystery creature fled across a stream and into dense forest. He also took a picture of what could have been its footprint. The date and time were logged as a few minutes past 11 am on 20 January 1993.

It wasn't much to go on. New Zealand's Department of Conservation expressed some interest but then pulled out following allegations from a friend of Freaney's that the whole episode was a publicity stunt. The friend, Dennis Dunbar, later withdrew the allegation, but the damage had been done.

Meanwhile computer enhancement of the photograph at Canterbury University gave the moa-spotters some support. Electronics department analyst Kevin Taylor said he believed the image in the photo probably was a bird, though it was impossible to specify a breed. Crucially, the creatures lower limbs were blocked by a rock.

There were several explanations offered by naturalists and scientists. Some thought it was a red stag, others a Cape Barren goose. One expert even claimed it was a couple of hikers. No one seemed prepared to accept that a species believed to be so long extinct could have continued breeding unnoticed in the wilderness of the Craigieburn forests.

Despite this scepticism, there have been numerous moa sightings across South Island within the last 100 years. In 1896 schoolboys reported seeing a moa crossing the road at Murchison. In 1928 three were seen at Preservation Inlet on the extreme south-west tip of the island. And in 1963 a scientist spotted a 'moa-like bird' in the north-west Nelson bush.

To add further intrigue to Freaney's account, two German tourists made a bizarre entry in the 'intentions book' kept at a hiker's hut near Brealey, on the Cragieburn range. The huts are scattered across New Zealand's bush to provide shelter for walkers.

In the book the Germans, Franz Christiansen and Helga Umbreit, made an entry for 19 May 1992. They said they had been busy exploring the Cass-Lagoon Saddle area of Harper Valley – the same ground on which Freaney's party had seen the strange bird. Almost as an afterthought they added: 'We were very surprised to see two moas.'

Christiansen and Umbreit have never been traced. Though future moa hunts in the region are now a certainty, the mystery of the big bird is as elusive as ever.

Gloria Ramirez

The death of 31-year-old Gloria Ramirez is unique in the annals of medical history. Never before have doctors trying to save a life been knocked unconscious by the fumes seeping from their patient.

Exactly how the woman from Riverside, Los Angeles, became a walking gas chamber is likely to remain a mystery. So is the fact that while some nurses attending to her passed out, others carried on their work unaffected. The case adds up to an account stranger than the weirdest plot of any 1950s Sci-Fi B-movie.

On Saturday evening, 19 February 1994, Ramirez was brought in to Riverside General Hospital complaining of chest pains and breathing problems. She also confirmed to nurses that she was suffering from cervical cancer, as a consequence of which she was taking pain killers and an anti-nausea drug.

As the staff prepared her for a series of tests Ramirez collapsed from an acute cardiac arrest. Exactly 36 minutes after being admitted she was now the subject of a full-blown emergency. Death would follow within the hour.

Nurse Susan Kane was first to succumb to the gas emanating from Ramirez. She had been taking a blood sample when she noticed a smell like ammonia coming from her. The blood in her syringe also seemed to have be contaminated with tiny yellow or white flecks.

Kane collapsed. Dr Julie Gorchynski immediately took her place but then passed out as well. Seconds later the respiratory therapist Maureen Welsh keeled over followed by nurse Sally Balderas and one of her colleagues. The emergency room was by now beginning to look like a bomb had hit it. Yet, curiously, the only member of the medical staff who seemed totally unaffected was Dr Humberto Ochoa. He didn't even notice the fumes.

For a week Dr Gorchynski remained in intensive care at Loma Linda University Medical Center, Los Angeles, as scientists tried to understand what had happened to her body. She was suffering breathing problems and muscle spasms, conditions which lingered for months afterwards. In April she had to undergo major surgery to save her knees. The bones were somehow being starved of oxygen.

The other medic badly affected, nurse Balderas, suffered intense headaches, sleep deprivation, stomach ache and vomiting. Both she and Dr Gorchynski were diagnosed as sleep apnoea victims, a condition in which breathing stops temporarily.

Balderas told doctors that Ramirez 'had this film on her body, like you see on the ground at a gas station'. Tests indicated that the victims had suffered organophosphate poisoning. There were the same white and yellow crystals present in their bodies as had been reported in Ramirez's blood sample. But this conclusion produced more questions than it solved. For a start, Ramirez had not taken organophosphates as far as anyone could tell. Her family emphasised that whatever pain she had been in from cancer, she would never have committed suicide. She would never have abandoned her two children.

The senior medical co-ordinator for California's Department of Food and Agriculture, Peter H. Kurtz, said: 'I know of no organo-phosphate in use today that would cause the kinds of things reported in that hospital.'

The post-mortem on Gloria Ramirez took place on 24 February under the most extraordinary conditions. Pathologists wore anti-chemical warfare suits and gas masks, breathing apparatus and two-way radios. A mini TV camera, air samplers and sensors were poked into the body bag before it was lifted out of its air-tight aluminium coffin and all medical staff were prohibited from working longer than a 30 minute shift inside the morgue. It was almost as though they were dealing with an alien from outer space.

The medical cause of death – cardiac arrest caused by kidney failure, in turn caused by cancer – shed little light on the mystery. Unable to comprehend the bizarre events, the local Coroner's Office resorted to the hopelessly unscientific and inadequate explanation that the fumes emanating from Ramirez's body were nothing more than the 'smell of death'.

Just about the only believable theory so far submitted has come from Californian police sources. They allege that Ramirez was a some time drug user who got her kicks from Phencyclidine (PCP), also known as angel dust. This anaesthetic compound is manufactured in illegal laboratories across the state. Ramirez was known to frequent one of them.

Had she experimented by rubbing one of the chemicals used in PCP manufacture onto her body, perhaps by first dissolving it in a medicine called DMSO? DMSO, which has the characteristic of smelling differently depending on the body tissue of the user, draws substances into the bloodstream through the skin.

This could explain the film on her skin and the strong smell of ammonia. But it is a theory supported by few hard facts. The mystery of Gloria Ramirez looks likely to endure for many years yet.